MILLER'S
ANTIQUES
& COLLECTIBLES
The Facts At Your Fingertips

INTRODUCTION BY
Judith Miller
US CONSULTANT
Lita Solis-Cohen

Miller's Antiques and Collectibles
The Facts at Your Fingertips

First published in Great Britain in 1993 by Miller's
an imprint of Reed Consumer Books Limited
Michelin House, 81 Fulham Road London SW3 6RB
and Auckland, Melbourne, Singapore and Toronto
This 1994 edition distributed in the United States by
Antique Collectors' Club Ltd.
Market Street Industrial Park, Wappingers Fall, New York, NY 12590

Editor Janet Gleeson
US Consultant Lita Solis-Cohen
Art Editor Prue Bucknall
Special Photography Jacqui Hurst
Executive Art Editor John Grain
Production Fiona Wright
Indexer Hilary Bird
Art Director Tim Foster
Senior Executive Editor Frances Gertler

ISBN 1-85732-583-4

Set in Bembo
Typeset by SX Composing Ltd, Rayleigh, Essex
Origination by Scantrans Pte Ltd, Singapore
Produced by Mandarin Offset
Printed in Hong Kong

Cover pictures: an Izannah Walker doll in good condition, Central Falls, Rhode Island, patented 1873, $20,000; Pennsylvania painted and stenciled chest of drawers, c1830, $100,000-125,000; Philadelphia open armchair that once belonged to George Washington, $25,000-30,000; Cobweb Tablelamp by Tiffany Studios, similar piece sold by Barbara Streisand fetched $717,500 in 1994; Currer and Ives lithograph, $45,000-55,000; Rocking horse, American 1875-1900, $17,600 in 1990.
picture pages 1 & 2: a 19thC William de Morgan two-handled vase, William IV silver gilt dessert-spoons, 18thC Meissen porcelain figures, a Baccarat rose paperweight, an 18thC mahogany longcase clock by Samuel Guy, a pair of ruby slippers worn by Judy Garland, a 19thC French bracket clock, a Moorcroft baluster vase c1928, a 19thC Staffordshire pottery Toby Jug, an early 19thC yew armchair, a George III soup tureen and cover c1770, an 18thC mahogany bureau, a 19thC kazak rug, a Meissen slop bowl, c1730, two gauge 0 electric locomotives with pick-ups c1940, a Jules Steiner bisque doll, c1890, a silver caster by Matthew Cooper, c1703, a 17thC oak joint stool, a two-colour opaque twist wine glass c1765.

CONTENTS

INTRODUCTION

People become interested in antiques and collectibles for a variety of reasons. In my own case there was nothing in my background to suggest that I would – my parents had none. Indeed, my mother was of a generation which, for the most part, used to discard everything once it was old. However, as an impoverished student living in a run-down part of Edinburgh during the late 1960s I bought a few cheap, pretty plates from the local junk shops that I passed every day on my way to and from the university. To me they provided a far more attractive and unusual means of decorating the walls of my room than the posters favoured by my flatmates. In much the same way as many other people who inherit or buy the odd item of china or furniture, I then became increasingly intrigued as to when and where the plates had been made. Later still, I also became interested in their value. Were they now worth more than I paid for them?

While my first foray into the world of antiques did not realize any profit to speak of, this in no way detracted from the considerable enjoyment my purchases gave me. Indeed, over the subsequent years, almost every collector I have met has bought for pleasure rather than profit; the value of any particular piece usually being a side issue to the joys of researching it, tracking it down, buying it, holding or looking at it, showing it off and even the simple fact of owning it.

Nevertheless, during a period in which buying and selling shares on the stock market has sometimes been a bit like swapping deck chairs on the *Titanic*, antiques and collectibles have, for the most part, proved to be a good investment. This is undoubtedly one of the main reasons for the enormous ground swell of interest in the subject over the past two decades. Moreover, the prospect of finding a long-forgotten object gathering dust in the attic, or buying for a few dollars an insignificant-looking item at a garage sale, that at auction turns out to be worth a small fortune, lends to this fascinating leisure activity all the excitement of a treasure hunt.

People often ask me, how they can learn about antiques. Although there is no magic way of becoming an expert overnight, there's no great mystery to it either. Learning about antiques is great fun and the best way of going about it is to do what I did: visit museums and historic houses, read books and attend courses on the subject, look around antiques shops, markets, fairs and auctions and, above all, ask questions.

Museums and historic houses are a great place to start. Invariably they contain some of the finest examples of all manner of antiques and thus help you to get your eye in and learn when a piece looks right. However, don't try and take in too much at once. You'll learn far more quickly if you concentrate on one subject at a time.

There are numerous books on antiques and collectibles available today – many more than when I first became interested. The *Miller's Price Guides* and *Checklists*, for example, are particularly useful! Containing thousands of pictures of antiques they give you a pretty good idea of current prices and help to familiarize you with the language of antiques. Courses run by leading auctioneers, such as Christie's and Sotheby's, or local adult schools are also now widely available and offer courses in a particular subject. If you do decide to attend one, don't feel embarrassed about asking questions. I remember attending a weekend course on porcelain run by Geoffrey Godden a few years ago. Right at the end a man suddenly confessed he had been confused by much of what had been said over the two days; he didn't understand the continual references to hard- and soft-paste porcelain, or what the difference was between them – a crucial piece of information that could have been easily explained if only he had asked at the outset.

Many people also feel intimidated about striking up a conversation with a dealer when visiting a shop, antique show or market. However, as I have found over the years, this is one of the best ways of acquiring knowledge. Indeed, most dealers are only too happy to discuss a piece and answer a reasonable number of questions. But do be sensitive to the fact that dealers have to make a living. Pick a quiet moment when they're not busy.

Attending auctions, which are held once a week or fortnight in many parts of the world, gives you the opportunity to view an enormous range of antiques and also introduces you to the real nitty-gritty of buying and selling. Go to the sale previews, buy a catalog and, if you

are particularly interested in a piece, ask to see someone from the auction house and discuss factors such as its history, any damage and the estimated price. Also go along to the sale itself, even if you have no intention of buying, and write down in the catalog the prices pieces fetch as they go under the hammer. By doing this you will be able to compare estimates with realized prices, and gradually build up a feel for how the market is doing in particular areas.

By the time you have done all or most of the above you will have acquired a considerable amount of knowledge about the antiques you have become interested in. However, do bear in mind that we are not talking about an exact science here. For every rule there is an exception. For example, I once wrote an article confidently stating that all 18th-century sideboards had six legs. When this appeared in print it was accompanied by a number of illustrations, one of which showed a totally authentic piece with four legs! I have also heard three eminent experts in their field disagree vehemently over the authenticity of a piece of oak furniture. This is not an unusual occurrence and is very much part of the joy of antiques.

On a slightly more serious note, I've also seen so-called 'antique' furniture made up by modern craftsmen using old wood and traditional techniques. Some pieces are so well done it's nearly impossible to distinguish between the fake and an original. As someone once pointed out to me: there are more English oak refectory tables distributed around the world than there were houses in 16th-century England of a sufficient size to even get them in the front door. So, do be careful, especially if you are thinking of paying a lot of money for something. Most antiques dealers are both honest and honorable, but as in most spheres of business, there are exceptions.

The questions I am most often asked are: how much is something worth, or how much should I pay for it? Well, price is almost always determined by a combination of four factors: condition, age, rarity and desirability. Condition can be vital. After a pristine Steiff teddy bear went for $82,500 at Sotheby's a few years ago, Bond Street was inundated with gentlemen in pinstripe suits clutching their play-worn childhood companions. There was considerable disappointment when they were informed that they were, at best, only worth $75-150. Age is also obviously important, as the older something is the greater the likelihood few examples will have survived. However, the rarity of a piece does not guarantee desirability, and it is the latter that is the most important factor in determining the price something will fetch. For example, Roman glass is old, can be found in good condition and some pieces are quite rare. However, if it is not considered desirable it will sell for a very low price at auction. In other words, the old adage that a piece is only worth what two people are prepared to pay for it usually holds good.

Assessing the value of an antique or a collectible is more difficult in some areas than others. For example, a good quality 19th-century mahogany dining table and chairs by a well-known maker can be said to have an intrinsic value. Precedent says they will at least have held their value 10 years on. Much the same can be said for pieces of 18th-century porcelain or silverware. However, it is far more difficult to predict whether a 1950s Japanese plastic robot, a smashed-up Fender guitar once played by Jimi Hendrix (one recently fetched $52,500 at auction) or a John Paul Gaultier dress designed for Madonna will be worth in 30 years time the sort of sums of money the present generation are prepared to pay for them. Of course, trying to predict these things is very much part of the fun of collecting – provided, that is, you stick to the following rules: always buy the best piece you can afford, especially in terms of condition and rarity. Never buy anything you don't like or you can't live with – you may have to live with it for a long time before you can get your money back. In fact, as long as you know what you're buying and the price you pay is appropriate at the time, you probably won't go far wrong.

JUDITH MILLER

PERIODS & STYLES

DATES	BRITISH MONARCH	UK PERIOD	FRENCH PERIOD	GERMAN PERIOD	US PERIOD	STYLE
1558–1603	Elizabeth I	Elizabethan	Renaissance		Exploration	Gothic
1603–1625	James I	Jacobean		Renaissance (to c1650)		
1625–1649	Charles I	Caroleon	Louis XIII (1610–1643)		Pilgrim (1620–1700)	Baroque (c1620–1700)
1649–1660	Commonwealth	Cromwellian	Louis XIV (1643–1715)	Renaissance/ Baroque (c1650–1700)		
1660–1685	Charles II	Restoration				
1685–1689	James II	Restoration				
1689–1694	William & Mary			William & Mary		
1694–1702	William III	William III			William & Mary (1690–1730)	Rococo (c1695–1760)
1702–1714	Anne	Queen Anne		Baroque (c1700–1730)		
1714–1727	George I	Early Georgian	Régence	(1715–1723)		(from 1750)
1727–1760	George II	Early Georgian	Louis XV (1723–1774)	Rococo	Queen Anne (1730–1760)	
1760–1811	George III	Late Georgian	Louis XVI (1774–1793)	Neoclassicism (c1760–1800)		Neoclassical (c1755–1805)
			Directoire (1793–1799)		Chippendale (1750–1785)	
			Empire (1799–1815)	Empire (c1800–1815)	Federal (1785–1825)	Empire (c1799–1815)
					Classical (1805–1830)	
1812–1820	George III	Regency	Restauration (1815–1830)	Biedermeier (c1815–1848)		Regency (c1812–1930)
1820–1830	George IV	Regency				
1830–1837	William IV	William IV	Louis Philippe (1830–1848)	Revivale (c1830–1880)	Late Classical (1830–1845)	Eclectic (c1830–1880)
1837–1901	Victoria	Victorian	2nd Empire (1848–1870)		Revivals★	
					Arts & Crafts (1890–1920)	
			3rd Republic (1871–1940)		Eastlake (1890–1910)	
				Jugendstil (c1880–1920)	Art Nouveau (1890–1920)	Arts & Crafts (1880–1900)
1901–1910	Edward VII	Edwardian			Art Deco (1920–1940)	Art Nouveau (c1900–1920)

★ Revivals: Gothic (1840–1850), Rococo (1840–1865), Renaissance (1860–1975), Colonial (1876–1920).

PART 1

WHERE

TO BEGIN

AUCTIONS

Auctions are one of the most exciting ways in which to buy antiques. Here you will find almost every type of collectible; from objects worth millions, to boxes of bric-a-brac costing just a few dollars. But buying at auction is very different from buying in a shop or market, and can seem quite bewildering to anyone who has never visited a sales-room or bought in this way before. Auctions are not limited to the big city salesrooms. The New York branches of Christie's and Sotheby's sell the majority of the more expensive antiques sold in the US, but Skinner's in Bolton and Boston Massachusetts, Butterfield's in San Francisco and Los Angeles California, Leslie Hindman in Chicago, and a myriad of auctioneers in cities and in the country hold estate sales where you can often buy less expensive antiques and bric-a-brac. Others hold specialized sales of toys, dolls, glass, books, bicycles, posters and sports memorabilia.

BUYING AT AUCTION
- BUY THE CATALOGUE
- VIEW THE SALE VERY THOROUGHLY
- DECIDE ON YOUR PRICE LIMIT AND STICK TO IT

Most would-be collectors who overcome their initial misgivings and visit an auction for the first time, find themselves hooked on the exciting atmosphere of the salesroom. The large turnover of goods means that there is always a possibility of uncovering an undiscovered treasure – or "sleeper" as it is known in the trade – and provided certain basic guidelines are followed, auctions are still one of the best places to buy reasonably-priced objects of good quality.

Going to auctions regularly is also an excellent way of learning about your area of interest before beginning to collect. If you attend auction previews regularly and read catalogs carefully, you will soon acquire a sound knowledge and a feel for prices which will stand you in good stead when you begin to spend money on your collection.

BUYING AT AUCTION
CATALOGS

Before a sale is held, most salesrooms will identify the goods to be sold in a catalog. Whether it's a typed sheet or a glossy illustrated publication, it will list and number the objects in the order in which they will be sold. The numbers in the catalog, known as "lot" numbers correspond to those attached to each object or "lot".

Next to each catalog entry there may be a suggested price range, for example $50-100. These figures show the price the auction house expects the object to fetch, and are known as the "estimate". If there are no estimates printed in the catalog they may be posted in the salesroom, if not, ask the auctioneer. Estimates should only

Some lots contain more than one item, all these albums were sold together in a stamp sale.

ever be taken as a rough guide, they are never a guarantee of the price for which something will be sold. Ultimately any work of art, no matter how rare or valuable, is only worth at auction what two or more people are willing to bid for it, and it is this element of uncertainty that gives auctions their special appeal.

VIEWING THE SALE

About two or three days before the day of the sale, all the objects to be sold will be put on display, so that buyers can examine them; this is known as the "viewing" or "sale preview". It's very important to attend one of these preview days because on the morning of the sale, when the porters are getting everything ready for selling, it may be impossible to view properly.

At the preview you will notice that every object has been marked with its lot number which corresponds to the number in your catalog. Objects are rarely displayed in numerical order, so if something sounded fascinating in the catalog and you can't find it at the view, ask one of the salesroom staff to help you. That way you won't miss anything which has been badly displayed.

At larger auction houses pay careful attention to the wording of the catalog entry. Read the explanations at the beginning of the catalog,

which tell you the significance of words such as "attributed to", "style of", and "after". This catalog terminology is like a code which tells you the expert's opinion of the date and authenticity of a piece and will have an important bearing on its value. Ask to speak to the expert in charge of the sale if you would like more information about a particular piece.

Always examine very, very thoroughly any object on which you intend to bid, and make up your own mind as to its authenticity. Pay particular attention to the condition of the piece and take into account the cost of restoration, which may be considerable, before deciding on your bidding limit. Also bear in mind that an auctioneer's commission (usually 10%–15% of the hammer price – the price at which the object is sold in the salesroom), will usually be added to the hammer price.

Above Each lot should be clearly marked with a number.
Right Viewing before the auction takes place.

Viewing at an auction.

BIDDING

If after viewing the sale, you decide you might want to bid, find out if you need to register first. Some salesrooms will want you to fill in a form with your name, address and phone number before the sale; some issue a number for you to hold up should your bid be successful; others simply call out your name and you fill in a form at the time.

If you are not paying cash, ask whether a check or credit card will be acceptable as a method of payment. If you intend to spend a large sum of money you may have to supply bank references.

Some sales last for several hours; if the lots which interest you are towards the end of the sale and you don't want to sit through the whole auction, find out how many lots the auctioneer sells per hour (usually about 100) to work out roughly when your lot will be sold; but remember to allow yourself a bit of extra time so you don't arrive too late.

If you can't get to the sale you can usually leave a bid with the customer service representative, who will bid on your behalf.

When the sale begins, the auctioneer will call out each lot number to be sold and will start the bidding at a figure which is usually slightly below the lower estimate. As the people present signal to him by waving or nodding he will call out their bids in increasing sums, called increments. Depending on the value of the piece, the bidding could rise in $5s, $10s, $20s, $100s, $1,000s, or more, the increments increasing as the price rises. The auctioneer will indicate that the bidding is finished by banging a small hammer, called a gavel, on the rostrum, and recording the sale and the name or number of the successful bidder. People who have never been to an auction before often worry that an ill-timed cough or sneeze could be mistaken as a bid and land them with a masterpiece; ask anyone with experience of auctions and they will tell you that this is unheard of.

When you are bidding for the first time remember to make your bids clearly and quickly. In a packed salesroom it can be quite difficult to attract the auctioneer's attention, so don't be faint hearted: wave your catalog or bidding card and call out if need be. However, if the bidding is rising rapidly and the auctioneer seems to be ignoring you, don't worry; an auctioneer will usually only take bids from two people at a time, when one drops out he will look around the room for someone else to join in; if you are still within your limit that is your moment!

SELLING AT AUCTION

Taking a prized possession for sale at auction can seem every bit as daunting as buying; especially if you don't know the object's history or what it might be worth. You are, after all, taking along something you hope may be valuable, and quite possibly have treasured for a very long time. But although many would-be sellers are put off by the thought of rejection, auction houses offer a very useful way of finding out more about your property and their advice is nearly always absolutely free.

SELLING AT AUCTION
- TRY TO GET MORE THAN ONE VALUER'S OPINION
- PHONE TO MAKE AN APPOINTMENT IF NECESSARY
- AGREE ALL CHARGES BEFORE LEAVING YOUR PROPERTY FOR SALE
- FIND OUT HOW SOON YOUR PROPERTY WILL BE SOLD

WHAT IT'S WORTH

When you visit one of the larger auction houses you will have to line up and show your property to a receptionist who will decide which expert should be called to value it for you.

Before the auction house expert examines your property he (or she) will probably ask you for anything you can tell him about the object. The history of an object, known as its "provenance", can help enormously in its correct identification and valuation. Details which might seem insignificant to you can help a valuer, so if you know your table once belonged to Aunt Ethel who lived in Boston, and bought it at a local house sale then don't forget to say so. After careful examination the expert will probably tell you what he can about your object. This may be where, when and by whom it was made, as well as what he or she thinks it might fetch at auction.

Should you decide to sell, the specialist should also advise you whether a "reserve" price is necessary. A reserve is the minimum price for which the auctioneer may sell your property, and can act as an important safeguard if the sale turns out to be very poorly attended. You should also remember to ask the expert how quickly your property will be sold. If the property is of exceptional quality you may be advised to wait for a particular sale which will feature other good quality objects and attract better prices. Certain specialty sales are only held once or twice a year, and it may be that you could sell more quickly elsewhere.

THE COST OF SELLING

An auction house does not buy your property from you, instead it sells on your behalf. For this service you will be charged a commission and costs, such as insurance and illustration (when necessary).

An auction house expert giving an over-the-counter valuation.

ANTIQUES SHOPS

Antiques shops are among the easiest of places in which to begin learning about and buying antiques. They are less frantic than auction rooms, you can buy when you feel like it, and you don't have to compete with anyone else for the object of your choice.

There is an enormous variety of antiques shops, from elegant New York galleries to small country dealers. Obviously your choice will be determined to some extent by personal taste and how much money you have to spend. But as in any trade there are disreputable dealers as well as honest ones, and if you are an inexperienced buyer it is very important to pick a dealer who is both knowledgeable and trustworthy.

One of the best ways to find a reputable dealer is through trade associations like the NAADA and ADA (see p165). You can phone these organizations and ask for lists of local member dealers to be sent to you, free

> **BUYING FROM ANTIQUES SHOPS**
> - GET A DETAILED RECEIPT
> - DON'T RUSH, TAKE YOUR TIME
> - PICK A REPUTABLE DEALER
>
> *The National Antique & Art Dealers Association of America, Inc.*

of charge. If, on the other hand, you are wandering down your Main Street and about to enter a tantalizing shop, remember to look in the window or on the door first; a trade association sign is a good indication that the dealer has stock of good quality and also knows his subject.

Dealers who are members of organizations such as NAADA in America (or BADA or LAPADA in England) have to undergo a rigorous selection procedure, which assesses both their stock and knowledge. Once members they are bound to keep to a strict code of practice which offers you, the buyer, reassuring protection, especially if you are about to buy something costly for the first time. Member dealers are bound to tell you as much about the piece as they can; and this includes pointing out any restoration the piece may have had. If after buying something from a member dealer, you discover it is not genuine, the organization will themselves organize a panel of independent experts to investigate your claim and make sure, if it is upheld, you get a full and speedy refund. Remember that even the best-intentioned dealers can make a genuine mistake. But a good dealer will want you to come back so it's not in their interests to misrepresent a piece.

The ideal antique shop should not only be reputable, it should also have a welcoming atmosphere in which you do not feel intimidated or pressurized to buy. It is worth returning to a dealer you trust because as you build up a rapport with him he will probably be able to help you in a variety of

Below The Manhattan Metropolitan Antiques Center.
Right A general antiques shop, Brighton, England.

similar pieces at other shops or auction houses, to make sure the price is a fair one. It is almost expected to ask the dealer whether the price he first mentions is his "best" one. Don't feel embarrassed to do this, most are quite happy to haggle and will come down a little – one well-known London dealer even takes buyers to task if they **don't** ask for a discount!

Before you make your final decision, ask the dealer as many questions as possible about the piece. Find out how old it is, whether it's marked, what it's made from, who made it, where, and whether it has been restored.

If you decide to buy the piece, make sure you are given a full written receipt, which states the dealer's name, address and telephone number, together with the date the piece was made, a full description of it, the price you have paid, and the date of the purchase. It is very important to keep this receipt in a safe place. You will need it for insurance or in the unlikely event that the piece turns out not to be genuine.

ways. He might let you take things home "on approval". He may have a "buy back" policy, which means he will let you sell back to him the objects you bought from him for the price you paid for them (a useful way of upgrading your collection). He may also look out for special things to add to your collection, and give advice and condition reports on objects you have seen at auction. Above all, a friendly dealer is one of the best ways of learning, from the inside, about your chosen subject and the fascinating world of antiques.

BUYING FROM ANTIQUES SHOPS

Unlike buying at auction, there is no pressure to buy at a particular moment from a dealer, and this gives you plenty of time to decide whether you really want the object.

Before buying any antique do try to price

THRIFT SHOPS

Buying from a thrift shop is rather different from buying from an antiques shop, here you must decide for yourself on the age, value and authenticity of a piece. Nonetheless if you have a keen eye, they can be fruitful sources of inexpensive collectibles. Many junk shops buy their stock from house clearance sales and deceased properties where the entire contents were bought for a fixed sum. Thus you will probably find an enormous variety of different types of objects all for sale, usually for relatively inexpensive prices. Most of the items for sale in a junk shop will not be "antiques", but they are a good place to look for early 20th century furniture and decorative items.

SELLING TO AN ANTIQUES SHOP

Contrary to popular belief it is not always best to sell at auction. Selling to an antique shop has numerous advantages. Once you have reached an agreement with a dealer in an antique shop, you will probably be paid as soon as you hand over your property, and there will probably be no hidden deductions for commission, insurance etc. (see p28). Selling to a dealer saves waiting for the sale which may be several weeks away (and there is always a possibility that the object may be unsold) and waiting for payment after the sale (usually at least two weeks).

Before selling to a dealer, however, you do need to be sure of the value of your property. The public nature of auction sales means that objects of value should always realize their potential value, even if the auction house appraiser has under-esti-

> **SELLING TO ANTIQUES SHOPS**
> ● FIND OUT WHICH SHOPS SPECIALIZE IN YOUR TYPE OF PROPERTY
> ● TRY TO GET MORE THAN ONE OFFER BEFORE SELLING
> ● NEVER SELL TO ANYONE WHO TURNS UP UNINVITED AT YOUR HOME

mated them. In selling to a dealer you have no such safeguard; you get the price you agree, no more and no less.

Do a little research before offering your property for sale and find out which dealers specialize in the type of object you are offering. You are far more likely to be quoted a fair price for a Victorian chair if you take it to a dealer in 19th century furniture, than if you show it to an 18th century specialist.

If your property is too large or difficult to take to the dealer's shop, many are very happy to visit you in your home, although do make sure you pick a reputable one (see p16) before inviting him in.

There is an old adage about dealers with more than a little truth in it: if there were four dealers and one Chippendale chair on an island, all the dealers would make a living! Don't be surprised if you are offered a wide range of prices for your property as you do the rounds with it. A dealer's offer will, to some extent, be dependent on what he thinks he can sell it for, and remember he has to make a profit or he would not be in business.

KNOCKERS

Never open your door to any "dealer" who calls uninvited, or who puts a note through your door telling you he pays cash for valuables and will return a day or two later. Many of these so called "knockers" are not to be trusted; their aim is to trick owners into selling their property for much less than its true value – so treat them with caution.

Opposite An antiques emporium, Portobello Road, London.
Below A variety of decorative 19th and 20th century ceramics for sale.

ANTIQUES SHOWS & MARKETS

Visiting antiques markets and fairs is a fairly effortless way of seeing a large number of dealers together and gives you a useful opportunity to compare their stock, and its quality and price. You can find out where and when they are held from local papers and antiques magazines. There are several different types of antiques markets and fairs:

● Large "vetted" fairs – where dealers from here and abroad take booths and every exhibit is checked to make sure it is genuine.

● Shows and markets where anyone can rent space.

● Permanent markets where specialist dealers congregate with shops or showcases every day, or several days a week.

● Weekly street markets where small traders sell antiques and collectibles from the early hours of the morning to other dealers, as well the general public. To catch the bargains, arrive early!

VETTED SHOWS

At a large antiques show you will probably have to pay an admission charge; for this you may be given a catalog which lists the various dealers exhibiting and their specialities; if not, such catalogs will usually be available to buy. Many of the larger shows which are held on a regular basis protect buyers by "vetting" all the exhibitors and their stock. This means that before the fair opens, a panel of experts on each subject will examine the items for sale in each booth to make sure they are authentic. At the best fairs, the vetting is an extremely rigorous procedure and even the most eminent dealers have been known to quake when the panel arrives at their booth!

Most larger fairs operate a "dateline", which means only objects made before a certain date may be exhibited at the fair. The datelines will usually be mentioned in the

The British International Antiques Fair at the National Exhibition Centre, Birmingham.

catalog, but they may vary for different types of collectibles. For example, pre-1900 for furniture, but pre-1930 for ceramics and pictures.

Large shows usually feature a wide variety of different types of collectibles, so you will find furniture, silver, ceramics, jewelry, textiles and much more, under one roof. There are also annual specialty fairs which concentrate on one particular collecting area; silver, ceramics, ephemera, and even dolls all have their special fairs. If you are a serious collector such events can offer a golden opportunity to meet leading authorities in their field, who may come from other parts of the country and otherwise be difficult to visit.

If you find yourself bemused by the bustle of the fair, don't be afraid to ask for a dealer's card, and arrange to visit them at their premises after the event. All dealers see fairs as a way of meeting new collectors and forging new contacts, as well as making sales.

OTHER SHOWS

There is a world of difference between the large vetted shows, and a plethora of smaller antiques fairs held in church auditoriums, school gymnasiums and fire halls in all parts of the country. Here you may still be charged an entrance fee, but there will probably be no fancy catalog and no dateline or vetting of the items offered. Many of the objects for sale may be better described as second-hand rather than antique, but nevertheless, provided you realize that you must satisfy yourself of the authenticity of anything you buy, such events can prove entertaining for a browse, and are sometimes a good place to buy inexpensive bric-a-brac and decorative items – and you may find a bargain.

Portobello Road, London.

MARKETS

Throughout the country there are many permanent antiques markets, malls and group shops where many dealers rent space under one roof. In some cities and towns there are a cluster of shops on a particular street. Seasonal week-long markets in Brimfield, Massachusetts have become tourist attractions for an international audience. At these markets dealers often buy and sell to each other as well as to collectors and provided you are confident enough in your particular field of interest, such markets can be good sources. It is always important to get a written receipt with the dealer's name, address and a description of your purchase.

Highly reputable specialist dealers often choose to operate from permanent antiques markets. Visiting such markets can be a good way of discovering dealers who have unusual types of collectibles fairly priced. A non-specialist may be inclined to over-value an object with which he or she is not familiar, a specialist will know precisely what it is worth and be competitive with other local dealers.

Throughout the country, and especially in London, there are also weekly markets where you can buy antiques. One of the

from, always get a written receipt, with the dealer's name address and a description of your purchase on it (see p16).

SELLING AT FLEA MARKETS

Throughout the country, in the warmer months there are outdoor weekly flea markets, generally on the weekends. If you have a considerable quantity of suitable items you

The Garage indoor antiques flea market, New York (top); the Manhattan Metropolitan Antiques Center (left).

largest and most fascinating is held in Bermondsey in the East End of London. The weekly markets in Adamstown Pa. and New York City are legendary (see pp164–165).

BUYING FROM FAIRS AND MARKETS

Whatever type of fair or market you buy

might want to take a table at a local flea market. If you have very few pieces selling direct to a dealer might be your best bet. To sell in this way find a dealer who is selling things similar to yours and go early when the market is quiet. If you don't sell at your first table be sure to pack your treasures away carefully before you go on to the next.

TAILGATE SALES

Recently, a buyer at a tailgate sale spotted some appealing pottery rabbits and bought them for a few dollars (see illustration on p11). The new owner then took her bunnies to an auction house for an expert opinion. They were immediately identified as being rare early examples of the Royal Doulton *Bunnykins* series and sold soon after for nearly $6,000. Such stories are not everyday occurrences, but the mere fact that they happen at all ensures the growing appeal of the tailgate sale.

Weekly flea markets are held in fields, car parks and play grounds in big cities and small towns. They may be advertised in trade papers and magazines, the local press or simply by notices pinned up in the area. Some are regular events, held every Sunday, others are held only in summer, or just once a year.

The flea market is a good way of emptying the contents of your attic or garage and reach more people than at a garage or yard sale. For a small admission charge anyone can fill their van with unwanted property and sell it for whatever they can. You can buy and sell almost anything at a flea market – old furniture, clothes, books, electrical equipment – you name it! If you are a collector of modest means, these sales provide an ideal opportunity to buy relatively inexpensive collectibles, but you have to be determined enough to sift through the heaps of uninteresting objects to find the tantalizing but elusive treasures.

BUYING AT A FLEA MARKET OR TAILGATE SALE

If you are about to visit a flea market for the first time there are a few simple guidelines which could help to make your day more successful.

First, remember to arrive early. This way

Brimfield Markets (above and below left).

you will get the pick of the goods. Start before dawn and take a flashlight along; you'll need it to see what's for sale. Remember to take cash with you, preferably in small bills. You can't expect people at most flea markets to welcome checks, nor to have unlimited amounts of change (though some dealers take credit cards). Keep your cash in a fanny pack or something similar, not only for the sake of security, but also because that leaves your hands free to examine the goodies!

If you do see something which takes your fancy, ask its price, but feel free to haggle over it. Bear in mind that there are no fixed prices at a flea market, the objects for sale are only worth what someone is willing to pay for them.

SELLING AT A FLEA MARKET

Careful planning and preparation are the key to successful selling at a flea market. Figure out what you are taking, and if it will all fit in your station wagon or van. Remember to allow space for a display table, (a wall-papering table or picnic table would be ideal) and a collapsible chair. When you pack the car, try to pack the table on top, so that you don't have to unload everything on to the ground before being able to get the table out! Some markets provide tables.

If you want to price things, do so clearly with sticky labels or tickets. Put on the price you would ideally like to receive, but be prepared to come down a little from this figure if need be. Remember to pack anything fragile with plenty of wrapping: bubble wrap and cardboard boxes are best for china and glass etc. Old blankets are useful for wrapping round pictures and prints.

Wear suitable clothes: rainwear and boots are often a good idea if the sale is in a muddy field. Take some sandwiches and a thermos of tea or coffee so you are extra well prepared for your day. Allow plenty of time for the journey, and try to arrive early so you get a good position where the maximum number of buyers will spot your goods early on, before they have spent all their money somewhere else. Don't worry if dealers rummage in your van while you're unpacking – it can be disconcerting but it's a good way to "break the ice"! Try and take some spare change with you, (keep it safe in a purse belt) and avoid checks whenever possible.

Finally, before the sale is over, try to arrange for a friend to come and help you. That will give you a chance to look at everyone else's offerings, and maybe spend some of your earnings at the same time.

Bargain-hunting at Brimfield Markets.

BUYING & SELLING FROM ADS

Advertisements are an alternative way of buying and selling antiques. You may find advertisements for antiques in a wide variety of publications, from national newspapers, to specialist magazines.

One of the main worries with buying and selling through ads is the danger to your personal safety, and the security of your property. However, provided you take the necessary precautions to minimize risks, this can be an effective way of buying and selling antiques.

BUYING FROM ADS

If you're responding to an advertisement in a newspaper or magazine, try and find out as much as possible about the piece before you go to see it. Ask how big it is, what sort of condition it is in and the price.

If after all this you are still interested in the piece, make an appointment to see it. Find out the seller's name as well as his address, and his home phone number if this is not the one in the advertisement. Try to go with someone else; if you must go alone, tell someone where you are going, including the name, address and phone number of the person, and when you expect to be back.

When you see the piece, remember to examine it very thoroughly and make up your own mind as to its age and authenticity. If you decide to buy it, or if you have to leave a deposit, remember to ask for a written receipt, which includes the name and address of the person you are buying from and the date.

SELLING THROUGH ADS

Ads can be a good way of selling your property if you don't want to sell through a dealer or at auction, but first you must decide where to place your ad and how much your property is worth.

Your choice of publication will be dictated by both your budget and the value and type of your property. At a public library look for a publication which has a large number of objects similar to yours. If the object you are selling might be of interest to a particular type of collector, look at the specialist collectors' magazines, as these are usually relatively inexpensive to advertise in and will reach a wider audience of potential buyers than a more general publication. If, for example you are selling an old doll, you might well be more successful by advertising in a doll collector's magazine, than in your local paper. When you have narrowed the field down, you could try phoning the numbers in similar advertisements to see what sort of a response they have had.

Before you place the advertisement, find out what your property is worth. Show the object to a few reputable dealers, or take it to an auction house to get a good idea of what you could reasonably ask for it.

Word the advertisement clearly and succinctly, try to mention the age of the piece if you know it. You can either give a box number or your phone number for interested buyers to respond to, but don't mention your name and address because this might encourage burglars.

If you have left a telephone number, try to be in to take calls when the publication first appears, and be prepared to give callers a full detailed description over the phone. It is quite a good idea to take a deposit from anyone who says they want to buy the object but will come back at a later date to pay and collect it. That way you will ensure you do get paid and will not lose out on other potential buyers who may respond to your advertisement. Try to avoid checks; cash, postal money orders or certified bank checks are much safer.

PART 2

BRINGING

IT HOME

ABOVE UNWRAPPING A 19TH CENTURY CARRIAGE
CLOCK.

LEFT PORCELAIN DISPLAYED IN PURPOSE-BUILT
CABINETS.

VALUING & INSURING

No collector enjoys contemplating the thought of losing a prized possession, but unfortunately, an unpleasant aspect of collecting antiques today is the growing risk of burglary. One result of the increasing number of art and antiques thefts is that most insurance companies now demand a professional written valuation to cover objects worth more than a certain amount.

If you are beginning to buy antiques you will certainly know what each piece is worth, and whether you need an appraisal. But supposing you bought them a decade or more ago, or have been given or inherited them, do you really know what they're worth, and for what sum they should be insured? In recent years, many types of antiques have risen in value dramatically. Numerous, once modestly-valued objects are now worth substantial sums, so if you're unsure as to the value of your collection, and whether you need an appraisal, it's a good idea to take professional advice. Remember, although an appraisal will involve some expense, if you don't have your possessions valued you could find that in the event of burglary or accident, you are inadequately insured and unable to replace your property.

VALUATIONS

There are various ways of having your antiques valued. If you know a friendly local dealer, and only have a few items, he may be able to provide you with a valuation, although you should check with your insurance company that this will be acceptable. If you have a fairly extensive collection, your insurance company may prefer a valuation from a specialist appraiser, or one of the larger auction houses, which has a large appraisal department.

One of the main advantages in using an auction house is that although most of the valuing will be done by "generalists" (valuers with experience in assessing many different types of antiques) if there is anything unusual in your collection, or anything they are unsure of, they can call upon specialist experts for advice. Every year an

Opposite A Japanese *cloisonné* vase c.1910, discovered by one of Bonham's insurance valuers. Its owner thought it was worth around $3,000. The vase was identified as the work of one of Japan's most prominent *cloisonné* craftsmen, Kyoto Namikawa, and later sold for over $90,000.

Below Valuation documents are required by increasing numbers of insurance companies.

amazing number of valuable treasures come to light when auction house valuers visit collectors' homes. Among the most extraordinary finds of recent years, are a priceless Ming bowl being used for the dog's water, and a medieval bronze employed as a door stop! Both of these were later sold for several thousand dollars.

THE COST OF AN APPRAISAL

Before you decide on who to call in to value your property, shop around and look for the best deal. Prices for appraisals vary, and can be calculated in various ways. It is best to get a daily or hourly rate, or a flat rate, not a percentage of the total value of your property (usually between ½% and 1½%). As a general guide, a valuer will be able to assess between 100–300 pieces per day. To some extent the fee you are quoted for your valuation will depend upon how much the auction house wishes to secure you as a client. To an auction house, a valuation is recognized as being an important way of establishing loyalty with their firm. So the chances are that if you have an unusually extensive collection say, of Tiffany glass, the auction house will be keen to lure you to their firm, and may be prepared to negotiate. You should always make sure you agree on the final figure before the valuation takes place, not afterwards. Some auction houses offer an added bonus by reducing their commission rates, should you decide to sell any of the items they have valued within a reasonably short period.

Whoever carries out your appraisal, you should make sure it includes a full description of every item, together with its dimensions and value for insurance purposes. The value placed upon each object will to some extent depend on where you would go to replace your property; would you go shopping in New York, or at your local auction house? The price an insurance valuer puts on your property will probably be at least 20% higher than what you could expect to get should you decide to sell. If you feel this will make your insurance premiums prohibitively high, you can opt for "market valuations" — in other words auction prices — instead. But bear in mind if the valuation is too low you could find yourself unable to replace lost items satisfactorily.

INSURING

Your appraiser may be able to advise you on selecting a suitable insurer for your collection. One way of reducing premiums is to shop around. If your collection is moderately large and valuable you will probably find it is less expensive to insure through a broker specializing in art and antiques. Whereas a large insurer will usually lump together your antiques in the general household policy, a specialist broker will assess the risk of different categories of antiques individually, therefore reducing premiums. Usually furniture and large items are less expensive to insure than small, easily portable items.

SECURITY

Being aware of the dangers to your collection is the first step in protecting it from various risks. When placing an object you must consider its materials and the possible damage from sunlight, moisture, radiators and working fireplaces. You should also be sure to place objects in stable displays and hang pictures with hooks that can bear more weight than you need, taking extra precautions if you are in an earthquake area.

Theft of art and antiques can either be targeted – thieves who are actually after your antiques – or almost by accident, an opportunity seized where the burglar who was looking for a television takes the art and antiques too.

For the first type, an important element of protection is privacy. Do not allow magazines to identify you if they publish photographs of your collection; if you lend to exhibitions, lend anonymously, be discreet.

For both types, your security system, used correctly, can help enormously. You can deter potential break-ins with perimeter devices such as lighting, window bars and electronic alarm devices. Interiors can be protected with modern detectors. For advice, your police department may have a Crime Prevention Unit that gives consultations. Your insurance company will also give indications of what is most effective by reducing premiums according to what security you install. Choose something you will use all the time. If your cat sets off motion detectors and you therefore will never turn the system on, it is totally useless. Numerous products which indelibly but invisibly mark antiques are constantly touted as elements of theft protection. Actually they can only help if the property turns up, and when it does, it may help to identify it as yours. This can be satisfactorily achieved without any technical aids.

> **HOW TO KEEP GOOD RECORDS**
> - PHOTOGRAPH AGAINST A PLAIN BACKGROUND – WHITE OR GREY IS USUALLY BEST
> - TRY AND FILL THE VIEW FINDER WITH THE IMAGE
> - PUT A RULER BESIDE EACH OBJECT TO GIVE AN IDEA OF SCALE
> - PHOTOGRAPH MARKS, CHIPS, DENTS, SCRATCHES

PREPARING FOR THE WORST

If you do become an art and antiques theft victim, you will be well prepared if you have documented your collection. It is virtually impossible to do this after the theft. Without a detailed catalog to identify your property, you will have little chance of recovering it even if the police find it!

You must be ready, quickly to provide the basic information about your stolen items. Keep a duplicate of the catalog of your collection off the premises. Both the police and the Art Loss Register need similar information: a photograph(s), dimensions and medium, when appropriate the artist and date of the work. Any remarks on the condition that are specific to your items can be considered as birthmarks and are very useful in identification. Report to the police right away. If the value is over $5,000, the FBI will be ready to believe it may cross state lines; ask your local police to bring in the FBI which is listed in your telephone directory.

Your insurance company comes next; they need the police report to start with.

Then contact the International Foundation for Art Research (IFAR) in New York City ((212) 879-1780) to register the items in their image data base and in the Stolen Art Alert section of their monthly magazine "IFA Reports". This organization has been working to curtail the sale of stolen goods since 1976. The Art Loss Register is a central source of information on what is stolen. Dealers, auction houses and law enforcement call in regularly to inquire if specific works being offered are stolen property. If someone asks about your stolen items, the Art Loss Register will notify you immediately and set the wheels in motion for the recovery of your property.

If you are insured by a company that subscribes to the Art Loss Register's service, the registration fee of $40 per item is covered: a small publication fee (currently $25 an item) is charged to catalog and illustrate your theft in "IFA Reports".

PHOTOGRAPHING

Photographing your property will enable you to identify items as yours in the event of a burglary. You don't need an expensive camera, just follow a few simple rules:

- use a plain background, white is usually best unless the object is white
- photograph outside if possible as natural light gives clearer definition
- compose the picture so that the object fills the frame (without cutting off any part)
- if necessary take the piece from more than one angle and photograph any marks or identifying features
- draw small or indistinct marks separately.

Remember to keep your photographs together in a safe place, and keep copies somewhere else for safekeeping. If you have a video camera, make a tape of your collection.

DOCUMENTING

Documenting your collection means keeping a record of every collectible object as you acquire it. It's a good idea to keep your records of each item in your collection all together in an inventory book. Then as your collection grows you will find you have a useful source of reference as well as a reminder of how your collection began.

Keeping a detailed record of each object in your collection is also an ideal way to show proof of ownership in the event of an insurance claim. So any new purchase should be documented, and photographed as soon as possible after you have brought it home.

To begin your inventory of your collection make a list of every object you wish to include. Then for each object write down the following information:

- Where it came from.
- The date you bought or acquired it.
- The price you paid for it.
- A full description of the piece, including its size, what it is made from, and any decorative features.
- A report of its condition, including cracks, chips, alterations or restoration. This should be updated whenever you have the piece restored.

Keep the receipts of anything you have purchased with the inventory.

A detailed inventory of your collection is invaluable when claiming against burglary or damage.

DISPLAY

Antiques can be displayed in a multitude of different ways, but it's important that the method you select should be appropriate to your lifestyle. You may long to display your collection of antiques throughout your home, but if, for example, you have pets, or small children, fragile, or potentially hazardous objects should be kept well out of harm's way – perhaps on a shelf or in a cabinet out of reach. Bear in mind that not only can children or pets damage vulnerable and valuable objects, but antiques can also pose a threat to their safety. Even something as seemingly innocuous as an old teddy bear may contain wires that could harm a small child.

However, so long as you take simple precautions, there's no need to feel frightened of your collection. Many types of antiques, such as furniture, glass and silver, can still be used for their original purpose, or adapted for modern day living. Successful display should allow you to enjoy your collection as much as possible, whilst still conserving it in good condition.

Before you decide where to put your antiques, you should bear in mind how the piece was originally intended to be seen and used. Some pieces of furniture, for instance, were made to be placed against a wall, others were meant to be free standing. Try and display the piece in an appropriate manner. If you have a smaller object, for example, a sculpture, which is meant to be seen from all the way round, and you have nowhere suitable to put it, you could place it

in front of a mirror, so it can still be appreciated from every angle.

You may find you need to have shelves or cupboards specially constructed to house your collection. However, before you decide where to install special fittings, don't forget that nearly all types of antiques, with the exception of ceramics, silver and metalware, should be displayed away from direct sunlight and direct sources of heat (see p34). So don't, for instance, display your samplers in front of a sunny window; and keep antique furniture away from heat ducts. If your room is a particularly sunny one, objects such as textiles and prints can be displayed behind non-reflective, light-resistant glass, which will allow you to enjoy them while protecting them from fading. If you need to mount old photographs, or printed ephemera, in order to display them behind glass, use mounting tape rather than glue which can irreversibly damage the objects themselves.

If you have a collection of vases or plates, or glass, you may consider having a series of small brackets built to display them. Make sure, however, that they all sit securely on their perches. If you are displaying plates on brackets, they will need to be propped up on plate stands. Before climbing up to put them in their final resting place, it's a good idea to test them on their stands at an accessible height, so you can check they are firm and unlikely to roll off. Plates and plaques can also be hung on a wall by using a wire and spring plate rack. These come in a wide variety of sizes, so make sure you choose the right one; if it's too small it could put the plate under strain and cause it to crack, and if it's too large the plate could fall down. To check the size is right put the hanger on top of the rack, it should be about 1 inch smaller than the diameter of the plate before you stretch it.

Shelves are also an effective way of displaying a wide variety of antiques. If you are planning to put several heavy objects on a shelf, make sure it's suitably strong, take advice from your builder if necessary. Don't forget that objects which are openly displayed will need periodic dusting, so it's no good putting them somewhere where it will be impossible for you to reach them from time to time. If you don't want to have to dust so often, consider putting your collection in a glass cabinet or display case – lockable ones are a good idea.

Small antiques are often more effectively displayed together, rather than dotted around a room. If you have a collection of small silver objects or boxes it might be a good idea to display them on an attractive tray, a dish, or even on a small table.

Antiques of different types look very attractive when displayed together, but always be careful before standing objects directly on top of old furniture. Silver and metal objects, particularly pieces with feet, can scratch the surface of furniture, so if in doubt stick felt pads to the bottom.

Among the many aids to the effective display of collections of antiques are pedestals, stands and hangers. Most of these can be purchased through department and hardware stores. Other specialized pieces of display equipment are available by mail order through specialty magazines.

Finally, once you've displayed your col-

Opposite Blue and white vases displayed on brackets.
Above A collection of porcelain displayed in an alcove.

lection, don't forget the importance of lighting it effectively, but bear in mind that if you place objects too close to powerful lighting they may be damaged by the heat. Nevertheless, a carefully positioned spotlight on your display will invariably create a dramatic focal point in any room, whether it's a cluster of plates on a cottage wall, or a group of priceless porcelain on the mantelpiece of a mansion!

CARE & RESTORATION

Looking after your antiques correctly is essential if they are to remain in good enough condition for future generations to enjoy as much as you do. Nevertheless, there is a world of difference between correctly caring for an antique and attempting to restore it to mint condition. Nearly all antiques reflect their age and you shouldn't expect them to look too perfect.

Porcelain restoration at West Dean College, Sussex.

In general, restoration reduces value; a piece with limited wear and tear will nearly always be preferable and more valuable than one which has been over-restored. Nonetheless, if your antique is in danger of deteriorating further because of the damage it has sustained, or if its imperfections are impairing your use and enjoyment of it, it may benefit from limited restoration. If this is the case, always consult a specialist restorer. Unskilled restoration can cause irreversible damage to an antique and may greatly reduce value.

Nearly all antiques, apart from silver, ceramics and glass, should be protected from direct sunlight and heat. Sunlight causes textiles, carpets, prints and furniture to fade. Direct sources of heat cause many substances, including wood and *papier mâché* to expand. This may lead to warping and splitting in antique furniture, and can cause cracking or flaking in pieces made from a *papier mâché* core with a painted surface.

Prolonged exposure to cigarette, pipe and tobacco smoke can cause discoloration in many types of antiques which can be tricky to restore. So always keep antiques in a well ventilated room, and protect them from excessive smoke.

Some general guidelines for caring for the main categories of antiques are listed below, other tips on caring for specific types of collectables are contained in Part 3.

FURNITURE

- Excessively dry conditions can cause veneers to lift, and joints to dry out. If your home is very well heated it may be worth investing in a humidifier to protect your furniture. Excessively damp conditions are also detrimental to furniture as the wood may rot.

- If pieces of veneer break off don't throw them away; keep them safely as it's always preferable to use original veneers and they will reduce the cost of restoration.

- Avoid silicone polishes and aerosol sprays; instead use a small amount of good quality wax polish from a tin or jar. Don't over-polish or the piece will become sticky.

- Never drag furniture when you want to move it as this causes strain on the legs – pick it up instead. Don't risk picking a piece up by its carrying handles (these are usually more decorative than functional), or by the top if it has a protruding rim; always support the main structure.

CERAMICS AND GLASS

When ceramic pieces are cracked or damaged, the current trend is to leave damage showing, rather than attempt to disguise it completely. Cracked pieces may be stuck together with a suitable glue, but they should not be overpainted. Chips may be filled and coloured to match, but should not be overpainted.

Restoration department at Sotheby's, London.

- Pottery, porcelain and glass can be cleaned occasionally, by hand, with warm soapy water and should be rinsed well before drying. Decanters should be stored with their stoppers off.
- Don't secure loose lids or stoppers with adhesive tape or adhesive paste as these can damage original gilding and enamel.

SILVER

Contrary to popular opinion, silver doesn't tarnish especially rapidly unless it's kept in a particularly damp atmosphere. Any commercial silver polish may be used and a toothbrush may be handy to remove polish from nooks and crannies. Always make sure that you remove all traces of polish, or it can clog up decorated areas. Don't overpolish silver, or you may erase decoration, and, eventually, wear the metal thin. You can wash silver, by hand, in warm soapy water. Don't put it in the dishwasher as the abrasive powder dulls the surface. Silver gilt doesn't need cleaning with polish; an occasional wash with soapy water should be enough.

- Don't over-polish Sheffield and electro-plate items as you will wear away the thin surface layer of silver.
- Never leave salt in cruets or cellars; salt may get under the glass liner and can cause corrosion spots.

CLOCKS

Most maintenance should be left to a specialist, although wooden cases can be carefully dusted and waxed occasionally. Brass and silvered dials are protected by lacquer and should never be polished or placed in contact with water or detergent.

- Cleaning and oiling the clock's movement should be carried out with great care by a specialist.
- Clocks with spring-drive and short pendulums can be carried from one room to another, but should be held upright. For long distance journeys the pendulum must be secured or removed. Longcase clocks should be dismantled before being moved.

CARPETS, RUGS AND TEXTILES

Carpets and rugs should be cleaned by brushing or beating (so long as they are not very frail).

- Placing a pad under an antique carpet will absorb wear and protect the pile.
- Sunlight can cause colours to fade and fibres to rot. Framed textiles can be protected behind special light-resistant glass.
- Unless they are very fragile, most textiles can be washed with warm soapy water.

PART 3

COLLECTOR'S
COMPENDIUM

ABOVE MEISSEN BLUE AND WHITE SHAPED
RECTANGULAR DISH, $3,000-7,000.

LEFT DOLLS AND TEDDY BEARS ON
DISPLAY IN AN ANTIQUES SHOP.

Of all the categories of antiques you can choose to collect, furniture is among the most popular and practical. Many pieces offer you the alternative of using them either for their original purpose, or of adapting them to modern day living. Furniture differs from other types of antiques in that you probably don't want to collect it by the type of object – nobody wants a room full of only chests or tables – but you may have an affinity for a particular wood, or style of decoration. Whatever your preference, you need to familiarize yourself with the styles, methods of construction, and types of material used, in order to determine whether the piece is "right" (in other words, in its original condition without any major alterations or additions) or "wrong" (some major change has been made to it, or it's a fake).

The following pages discuss some of the most common types of furniture you'll come across, and give you hints about what to look out for. Once you've read them, visit as many auctions and dealers as possible before you begin to buy. Don't be afraid to pull out drawers, get down on the floor and look under table tops, and lift up chairs to look at their legs. Remember there's no better way of learning about the subject than by hands–on experience!

BASICS

When deciding whether a piece of furniture is genuine, identifying the wood used, the type of construction, the decoration and quality of workmanship are all crucial in helping you to make up your mind.

WOODS
At first furniture was made from solid wood, but as cabinet-making improved, the technique of decorating furniture by applying veneers (thin sheets of wood) developed. This was an economical way of using expensive woods, and allowed the maker to create decorative effects from the different grains and patterns (called figuring). Veneered furniture has a carcass (solid body) made from a different (usually less expensive) wood. This secondary wood, is most commonly pine or poplar in the US. In America wood was abundant and solid wood was extravagantly used.

AMBOYNA
Richly colored rare wood with a tight grain, used during the 18th century, Regency and Art Deco periods, nearly always as a veneer.

BEECH
Brownish–whitish wood used in the solid from the 17th century for the frames of upholstered English furniture, because it doesn't split when tacked. Rarely used in the US.

CHERRY
Reddish-brown wood popular for American Queen Anne, Chippendale and Federal furniture including four poster beds. Usually used in the solid.

CHESTNUT
Ranges in tone from light to dark brown, much used during the 18th century for French provincial furniture made in the solid. Used as a secondary wood in Rhode Island.

EBONY
Dense, heavy, almost black wood, often used as a contrasting inlay in marquetry veneering.

ELM
Light brown wood, popular for English Windsor chairs and provincial English furniture.

MAHOGANY
Rich golden-brown or red-brown wood, used in England from c.1720 and in America from the 1730s. There are several types of mahogany, San Domingan, Cuban, Honduras and Spanish are most common.

MAPLE
Maple is a hard wood (called rock maple). A close grained, distinctly American wood used solid and as veneers in American chests and desks, and as a secondary wood underframing mahogany chairs in New England. Figured maple – so-called curly, bird's eye and tiger maple are freaks of nature. Turned maple is found in chairs and bed posts. The sap of this tree is used for maple sugar.

OAK
Deep rich chocolate-brown, or paler golden-brown coarse-grained wood used predominantly in Britain from Middle Ages to late 17th century and in America in the 17th century and again in the Arts and Crafts period in the early decades of the 20th century. Also used as a secondary wood on good quality furniture.

PINE
Pale honey colored wood used in England and America as a secondary timber for drawer linings, and in the 19th century for inexpensive furniture (usually painted). As a secondary wood, soft yellow pine was used in England; hard yellow and white pine was used in America.

ROSEWOOD
Highly figured dark red-brown wood with blackish streaks. Popular during the Regency and Victorian periods in England and in the Federal and Early classical and Victorian periods in America.

SATINWOOD
Light yellow-West Indian wood, favoured from the late 18th century in England and in the Federal period in America. Usually used in veneers as it was expensive. In England it was sometimes embellished with painted decoration. Painted satinwood furniture was also popular in the Edwardian period.

TULIP POPLAR
A native American hard wood distinguished by green bands. Easily worked; used as a secondary wood throughout the mid-Atlantic states.

WALNUT
Richly colored wood resembling mahogany. Used solid and as veneers on English and American furniture from 1660 on. Regarded as the most desirable wood during the Queen Anne period in America (1730-1760), but by the end of the period mahogany was gaining in popularity. A large amount of American or Virginia walnut was exported to England from c.1730 and became very fashionable.

YEW
Red-brown hardwood used both in veneers or in the solid on the best English provincial furniture of the 17th and 18th centuries.

COLOR AND PATINA
A rich mellow colur is one of the most important features of any piece of furniture. The **patina** is the glow the wood develops over the years from an accumulation of wax polish and dirt.
● Most furniture is not the same color all over – grooves and carving will look darker, surfaces exposed to sunlight may be lighter.

PROPORTIONS
The proportions of furniture are fundamental in assessing quality, and deciding whether a piece is "right".
● A piece which looks too heavy on top, or has legs which are too big or small may be a "marriage" (see p41).
● Small pieces are usually more desirable.

CONSTRUCTION

Early furniture was made using mortice-and-tenon joints held by pegs (below) instead of glue or screws. This method

was used throughout the 18th century. Pegs were hand-made and stand slightly proud of the surface.

● Later machine-made pegs are perfectly symmetrical,

and are either flush with the surface or slightly recessed.

● From the early 18th century joints were dovetailed and glued (above).

● Until the mid-19th

century in America, when the circular saw was introduced, all wood was sawed by hand and has straight saw marks. After c.1850 circular marks may be visible on the surface of unfinished wood.

SCREWS

The earlier the screw the cruder it will be.

● The groove on old screws tends to be off-center and the top irregular (above).

● The thread is also irregular and open and, unlike modern screws (below), runs the entire length of the shank.

DRAWERS

● Dovetails are the triangular joints which slot together on the corners of drawers. They became progressively finer (see p43) and can help with dating.

● Drawers had channels in their sides until the 18th century, and ran on runners.

● Some drawers ran on the dust boards and had no runners.

● From the Queen Anne period the runners were placed under the drawer at the sides and ran on bearers placed on the inside of the carcass.

HANDLES

● Handles can provide a useful clue to dating, because styles changed from period to period (see p42).

● It's common to find pieces with replaced handles; this isn't serious but it's preferable to have handles in keeping with the rest of the piece.

● From c.1690 in England and early 18th century in America, handles were secured by pommels and nuts.

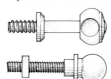

● Antique pommels were hand-cast in a single piece of brass (above). The thread goes only halfway up the shank, and

early ones taper slightly at the end.

● The nuts used to attach handles in the 18th century were irregular in shape. Modern nuts are regular, square or hexagonal.

FEET

Feet can give a useful guide to dating (see p42); however, centuries of standing on damp floors often causes feet to rot and many have been replaced.

● Compare the wood of the feet with that of the rest of the body to decide whether or not they're original. Undisturbed secondary wood blocks guarantees original feet.

LOCKS

● Early locks are usually of wrought iron held in place with iron nails. From the 18th century locks were steel or brass and secured with steel screws.

● Locks are often replaced; this isn't serious although pieces are more valuable with original fittings.

CARVING

Oak was relatively difficult to carve. As walnut and mahogany became popular carving became finer and more intricate.

- Original carved decoration adds to the desirability of a piece.
- Some pieces were adorned with later carving; these are far less desirable than those with original decoration.

VENEERING

The quality of veneering has an important bearing on price.

- Many pieces have *quarter-veneered* tops, where four pieces of wood create a pattern.
- *Banding,* strips of veneers laid around the edges of drawers, were also popular. Depending on the way in which the grain of the wood runs, banding is referred to as *straight banding, cross banding, feather* or *herring bone banding.*

INLAY/ MARQUETRY

A pattern made from veneers of differently coloured woods (see p44). Inlaying was popular on English and Continental furniture from the 17th century in England, c.1715 in America, and can add greatly to value.

CONDITION

Furniture in original pristine condition commands the highest prices and is always scarce.

- Don't dismiss pieces with blemishes – so long as the wood itself has not been damaged; surface spots can often be treated by a good restorer. The table (above) may look rather scruffy but the wood itself is undamaged and could easily be repolished.

WOODWORM

Small round holes in old furniture are a common sight especially in old English furniture and show that the piece has at some stage been attacked by woodworm.

- These need not put you off, provided the infestation has not caused structural weakness.
- Active woodworm can be detected by pale coloured powder in the worm holes, or on adjacent surfaces, and should be treated with a proprietary product as soon as possible.
- Check periodically for signs of infestation.

MARRIAGES

A piece of furniture made up from separate parts which did not originally belong together is called a "marriage".

- The married parts may be of a similar period or one part may be later, or even modern.
- Marriages are always much less desirable than pieces in original condition. In America replaced parts can drastically reduce value.
- Examine furniture in the way described on p38 to make sure it isn't a marriage.

ALTERATIONS

Furniture which has been altered is less desirable than pieces in original condition. Among the most common alterations are large pieces which have been reduced in size. Freshly cut surfaces, repositioned handles, and plugged holes are signs of alteration.

FAKES

A piece of furniture can be described as fake if it deliberately makes you think it's older than it really is. Fakes made from new timber are usually easy to spot as the wood doesn't have the patina of age you would expect. Fakes made from old wood can be more tricky to identify. Beware of any piece being sold as 18th century or earlier if it has circular saw marks (see p40). These mean the wood was cut after c.1850 when circular saws were first used. Specific types of fakes are dealt with in Part 3.

CHESTS

Chests of drawers are among the most indispensable pieces of furniture for storage and, not surprisingly, have been made in huge numbers over the centuries. They are still among the most easily available and inexpensive pieces of antique furniture – although of course there are rare and expensive ones as well.

A chest has many of the elements found in other types of furniture – drawers, feet, handles and so on – and if you want to learn how to date and authenticate any type of antique furniture, examining a chest carefully can teach you a great deal.

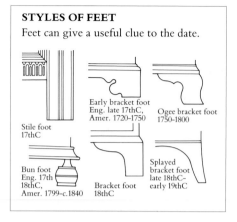

STYLES OF FEET
Feet can give a useful clue to the date.

Stile foot 17thC

Early bracket foot
Eng. late 17thC,
Amer. 1720-1750

Ogee bracket foot
1750-1800

Bun foot
Eng. 17th
18thC,
Amer. 1799-c.1840

Bracket foot
18thC

Splayed
bracket foot
late 18thC-
early 19thC

HANDLE STYLES

Eng. late 17th
-early
18thC, Amer.
up to 1750

Early
18thC

2nd quarter 18thC

2nd half
18thC

Eng. late 18thC
-early
19thC, Amer.
early 19thC

◀ ENGLISH WALNUT CHEST
Size has an important bearing on the price of all chests. Although this walnut veneered 18th century chest is in a sorry state, it's desirably small (30in wide) and so is still worth $3,000-5,000. Similar American chests, $4,000-6,500.

▼ ENGLISH MAHOGANY CHEST
Mahogany chests, such as this (c.1765), are more common than walnut ones and usually cost less (see above). $3,500-5,000. Small American chests $8,000-$12,000; larger $5,000-7,000.

WHY DO DEALERS LOOK IN DRAWERS?

Pull the drawer out and look for marks on the dustboards inside the chest – if the chest is original the marks of the runners should correspond with marks on the bottom of the drawer. From c.1790 drawers were strengthened by baseboards running from side to side with a central rib.

CONSTRUCTION

Examine the dovetails – they can tell you when the drawer was made. The earliest drawers have coarse dovetails; later drawers usually have more and finer ones. Don't just look at one drawer, check that they are all similar.

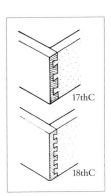

17thC

18thC

THIS MAHOGANY CHEST WAS MADE c.1790. THE BOW-FRONTED STYLE REMAINED POPULAR THROUGHOUT MUCH OF THE 19TH CEN-TURY. ENG. OR AMER. $1,000-4,000; WITH FINE VENEERS AND INLAYS UP TO $10,000+

HANDLES

Check drawers inside and out for marks, such as holes or an outline of a handle shape, where different handles might once have been. Don't be put off if the handles are replaced – it's very common.

UNDERSIDES

Don't expect chests to be neatly finished all the way round. They were made to stand against a wall and their backs and undersides are usually made from rough unpolished boards.

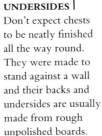

FEET

The feet are most prone to wear and are often replaced, so check the color and grain of each one. These feet are original and appropriately battered.

DRESSERS & CABINETS

In most collectors' minds antique cupboards epitomize "country" living and rustic charm. They give instant atmosphere to a room and can look equally impressive in a dining room, kitchen or hall. According to the type, cupboards vary greatly in price. Those made of simple pine in the 19th century are generally painted and those that have paint-grained decoration can be very expensive.

Generally, simple hard wood corner cupboards are more affordable. Scroll top high chests are distinctly American, used long after the English gave up the form. New England high chests often have simple fan carving while in the mid Atlantic states highly carved shells and grasses were favored. Generally, flat top high chests are more affordable than scroll top. High chests create a dramatic focal point in a room but you will have to dig deep in your pockets to afford one. Flat tops $10,000-100,000+, Scroll tops or closed bonnet tops $50,000–300,000+.

If you seek more affordable elegance, look out for 19th century cabinets made to display valuables. Called credenzas in England, many display cabinets are relatively inexpensive.

▼ CABINETS
This walnut high chest of drawers made in Philadelphia by Thomas Affleck c.1779 with swan's neck pediment ending in carved rosettes, and flame finials on fluted plinths is typical of Philadelphia. One of a documented pair with matching dressing tables; sold for $363,000 in 1985.

MARQUETRY

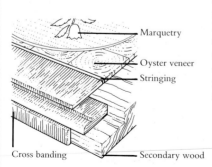

Marquetry
Oyster veneer
Stringing
Cross banding
Secondary wood

Marquetry decoration is rare in America, more common in England. It always adds to value. Terms used to describe different kinds of marquetry are:

● **Oyster veneering:** slices cut across branches to make patterns like an oyster shell.

● **Cross banding:** border with a grain at right angles to the main veneer.

● **Parquetry:** geometric pattern of small pieces of veneer.

● **Stringing**: narrow line of inlaid wood.

● **Floral**: marquetry designs of Dutch–influenced flowers.

WHAT TO LOOK FOR

Early (pre-1840) cupboards
- better ones have dove-tailed drawers
- step back cupboards – the top stepped back from the bottom, are more desirable
- American painted cupboards are desirable
- shaped boards and architectural moldings

WELSH DRESSERS

Beware of dressers where the base and rack have been "married" and did not originally belong together.

Compare the color and patina of the wood on both parts – here the color of rack and base are similar, showing that they belong together.

Look for the outline of the rack on the base, such as you can see here. $7,000–10,000. **REMEMBER** – not all dressers had racks.

▶ DISPLAY CABINETS

Victorian cabinets can still be bought for under $2,000, a bargain considering their usual good quality especially when you compare them with the cost of earlier, similarly elaborate pieces. This English one is worth $2,000–2,500 and has many desirable features: walnut veneers, original glass and gilt mounts. American examples c.1870 by known makers can be worth two to three times as much.

CHAIRS

Chairs are among the most essential pieces of furniture, and not surprisingly the finest, made in the 18th century or earlier, or by certain 19th and 20th century designers, can be very valuable. Prices for dining chairs are not only affected by quality and age but also by the number of chairs in the set – the longer the set the more expensive each chair becomes. But if you choose a simple pattern you may be able to find odd numbers of chairs and build up a set piecemeal.

The first chairs were simply constructed like stools, with a plank of wood at the back which sometimes had carved decoration. During the second half of the 17th century walnut replaced oak as the favorite wood and chairs were often elaborately carved with scrolls on stretchers and legs.

Mahogany chairs became popular during the 18th century, and chair styles reflected designs published by leading designers such as Chippendale, Hepplewhite and Sheraton. Their pattern books were widely circulated to cabinet-makers in England and America, who reproduced the designs, often in much simplified form. Nowadays, when a chair is described as "Chippendale", "Hepplewhite" or "Sheraton" it usually means it is based on one of their patterns rather than made by the cabinet maker himself.

DATING

18th C — leg, seat rail

corner block all just glued

block

19th C — leg, seat rail

corner bracket glued and screwed

corner bracket

Before the 19th century, chair seat frames were strengthened with glued corner blocks. In America the shape of the block determines where it was made.

▼ EARLY OAK CHAIR

Carving can help identify a chair's origins. This one dates from c.1640 and is carved with the dragon crest and scrolled arms typical of the Gloucestershire region. $1,500–7,000. A comparable American chair is very rare $100,000+ (one sold for $400,000, an aberration at the top of the market).

▲ WALNUT CHAIR

This c.1720 piece has characteristic cabriole legs and drop-in seat. The stretchers mean this was probably made by a provincial maker. $500+. A comparable American chair c.1740, with shells on knees and crest much higher $2,500–3,000.

THOMAS CHIPPENDALE

Many of Chippendale's chair designs featured pierced splats carved with scrolling foliage and incorporating Gothic elements, as seen on this *c*.1765 chair. Ribbons and chinoiserie details were also popular. $2,000

WHAT TO LOOK FOR

- Examine chairs carefully for signs of genuine wear and the patina of age – nearly all types have been reproduced at some time since the 19th century.
- If the color of one part looks very different it may be a replacement.
- Thick brown varnish often indicates a chair trying to look older than it is.

▼ REGENCY CHAIR

This *c*.1800 painted chair, with gilded decoration, slender arms and ebonized, tapered front legs is typical of the early Regency period. Later chairs have heavy proportions. $750–2,500. An American chair of mahogany similar design $3,000–5,000

▲ WINDSOR CHAIR

Made from woods such as elm, oak, ash and yew, Windsors usually date from *c*.1700. Yew Windsors, such as this, *c*.1810, are the most sought after. $750+. American Windsors have spindle backs and were painted to conceal different woods, often hickory, maple and poplar.

▼ BALLOON-BACK CHAIR

The value of this *c*.1860 Victorian walnut balloon-back chair is increased by its fine proportions and desirable needlework seat cover. $150–200. English or American.

ENGLISH CHAIR STYLES

The changing styles of chair backs, legs and feet can help collectors to date chairs. The sketches below show a selection of the more commonly-seen designs. However, as most of these were repeated in later periods, the style of a chair must be seen only as a guide to its age, not as proof of its authenticity.

1

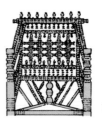
2

CHAIR BACKS
1. Early 16thC turned chair
2. Cromwellian padded
3. 17thC turned chair
4. Early 18thC Queen Anne chairs with vase-shaped splat
5. Ladder-back with horizontal pierced splats, c.1760
6. Chippendale chair with pierced and carved splat c.1760
7. "Chinese" Chippendale chair c.1760
8. Plain Chippendale chair with pierced splat c.1760
9. Late 18thC Hepplewhite shield-back
10. Late 18thC Chippendale chair with Gothic splat
11. Late 18thC lyre-back
12. Early 19thC country ladder-back
13. Late 18thC hoop-back with wheatsheaf splat
14. Sheraton square-back arm chair c.1790
15. Early 19thC Sheraton square-back
16. Late 18thC Gothic Windsor
17. Early 19thC spindle-back
18. Early 19thC bow Windsor
19. Regency with key pattern c.1820

20. Regency rope twist c.1820
21. Early Victorian c.1840
22. Gothic square-backed c.1830
23. Victorian Rococo Revival balloon-back c.1850
24. Victorian Jacobean late 19th and 20thC

LEGS AND FEET
1. 16thC baluster
2. Late baluster turned
3. Second half 17thC barley-twist
4. Inverted cup and trumpet c.1675-1700 (in Amer. 1710-1730)
5. Late 17thC double scroll
6. 18thC cabriole with pad foot
7. 18thC cabriole with carved scroll
8. 18thC shell carved cabriole with ball and claw foot
9. Early Georgian carved cabriole
10. Mid 18thC acanthus carved cabriole
11. Straight, fluted leg 1750-80
12. Blind fret, mid 18thC
13. Late 18thC turned spade foot
14. Early 19thC saber-leg or klismos
15. Victorian twist-turned
16. Mid-19thC reeded

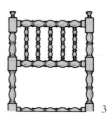
3

4

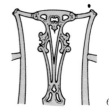
5

6

7

8

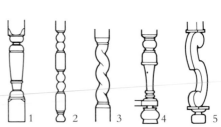
1   2   3   4   5

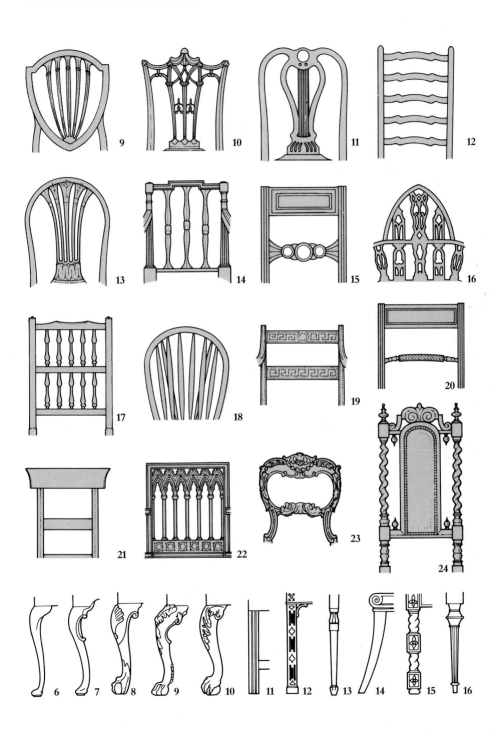

9

10

11

12

13

14

15

16

17

18

19

20

21

22

23

24

6

7

8

9

10

11

12

13

14

15

16

UPHOLSTERED CHAIRS & SOFAS

No home would be complete without comfy sofas and chairs, and antique upholstered furniture can be less expensive than modern counterparts. Though rare, American ones are selling for $2,500+. Three have brought more than $1 million!

Among the most popular types of chairs are winged armchairs with simple cabriole legs and side panels to keep out chilly draughts. These were first made in the early-18th century and the design has remained virtually unchanged to this day. The wooden frame is the most important part of antique chairs and sofas, so never buy a chair with a severely damaged frame. Damaged upholstery can usually be restored.

WING ARM CHAIRS

◀ **SIGNS OF AGE**
The marks of the original upholstery nails are clearly visible here and are a good sign of authenticity.

▲ **BEFORE**
Although this armchair (shown on the right after re-upholstering) looks terribly tatty, being able to see it like this is a bonus – you can make sure the wood is original and hasn't split or been weakened by woodworm.
● If the chair is recently re-covered, ask if there are photos of the frame.

▶ **AFTER**
It is very rare to find a chair with its original covering. If it exists it should be saved as a document, and fabric in a style appropriate be substituted. This 18th century chair is covered in silk damask; $7,000+. American wing chairs with cabriole rear legs are rare, $100,000+. With hairy paw front feet, very rare $200,000+.

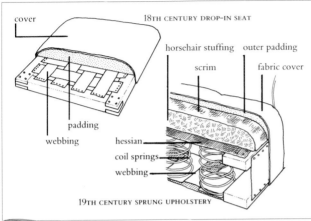

cover

18TH CENTURY DROP-IN SEAT

padding

webbing

horsehair stuffing   outer padding

scrim   fabric cover

hessian

coil springs

webbing

19TH CENTURY SPRUNG UPHOLSTERY

WHAT'S INSIDE A CHAIR?

Before c.1830 the upholstery on chairs was made from thin layers of horsehair and padding supported by webbing covered with fabric. Coiled metal springs covered with padding and webbing date from; in America from 1850.

▲ REGENCY RECAMIER

The outward curving "saber" legs, dark painted wood, and "anthemion" flower decorations are clear signs that this elegant chaise longue dates from the Regency period (c.1815). Although not very comfortable, Grecian couches or recamiers have become popular; this one could fetch $7,500+; if American $8,000–15,000.

◀ BUTTON BACKS

Before buying a Victorian button back, look for a manufacturer's mark or label underneath; these can add greatly to value – Howard & Sons' labels are especially desirable. This one is worth over $4,500, but you can find others from $2,500. A button back by a well known American maker could bring $7,000–8,000

DINING TABLES

PEDESTAL TABLES

Elegant pedestal tables are so practical and popular that they have been made continuously from the 18th century to the present day. Value depends largely on age and number of pedestals. A 19th century one such as this might cost from $6,000 upwards, a modern version $1,500–4,000. Not made in America until early 19th century; if American, worth three times more.

BEFORE YOU BUY IT . . . fit any extra leaves in the table to check they aren't warped.

SIGNS OF AGE

- solid mahogany to usually without crossbanding or inlay
- "reeded" edge to tops
- brass casters — plain or cast as lion's paws.

There are many different types of dining tables to choose from, depending on what size you require – and how much you want to spend. Remember to look at the grain of the wood on the top – an attractively grained top is a definite plus but will increase the price. If you're on a limited budget don't dismiss tables which have marked tops – so long as the wood has not been damaged it can probably be restored to its former glory. Don't forget to sit down at the table to make sure it is a comfortable height and the legs don't get in the way of yours.

WHAT TO LOOK FOR

- Signs of wear on the legs and top – scratches and marks are a sign of genuine age and to be expected.
- Legs of more or less the same color – if one is different it might be a replacement.
- Flaps which match the rest of the table reasonably well – those used only occasionally may not have faded as much as the rest of the table top but their figuring should be similar.

◄ REFECTORY
TABLES
Among the earliest
dining tables, most
date from the
17th-18th centuries,
but fakes exist, many
made from old floor
boards. Look for
circular saw marks –
these show the table
has been made or
tampered with since
the 19th century. This
one dates from *c*.1620
and is worth over
$15,000. No 17th
century American
ones with six legs
exist; with four legs
$40,000+.

► DROP LEAF
TABLES
Drop leaves with
simple pad feet like
this are among the
most affordable types
of 18th century tables;
this one would cost
around $1,500.
American examples
$3,000-5,000; smaller
and with cabriole legs
much more
expensive.

▲ D-ENDED
TABLES
Adaptable D-ended
tables come in several
sections; the ends can
be used as side tables.

$3,000-7,000.
American $6,000-
10,000, more with
inlay.

► GATELEG
TABLES
Hinged "gates"
pull out to hold up
the flaps on these
17th/18th century
tables – hence their
name. The most
expensive ones seat
six or more. $1,800.
American $15,000+.

BEWARE
Some tops are
"married" (see p41)
to different bases:
look under the top –
be wary of marks
which could have
been made by
different supports.
Feet are often
replaced.

SMALLER TABLES

Most of the myriad types of small tables date from the 18th century or later. Before this, side-tables were mainly general purpose and often rectangular in shape. As fashionable society became increasingly sophisticated, furniture became more varied and elegant and a wide range of small tables designed for specific purposes, such as tea-drinking, card playing or sewing, were made. Nowadays these can be just as useful for putting the telephone on as for their original function. Small tables fit easily into most modern homes so they have remained very sought after. Pairs are always especially desirable.

WHAT TO LOOK FOR

The decoration on better quality tables can add greatly to their value – the most desirable features are:

● carved decoration on legs and feet
● tops decorated with elaborate inlay made from differently colored woods or specimen stones
● painted decoration – popular in the late 18th century and the Edwardian period
● gilt metal mounts.

▶ TRIPOD TABLES
Carving is easily damaged and can be expensive to restore. The "pie crust" rim of this 18th century tilt-top table has been chipped. Price depends on size, $2,500+. American pie crust tea tables rare, $200,000

▲ CARD TABLES
The projecting circular corners of this 18th century table are stands for candles needed to illuminate cards and chips during play. $3,000+. American turret top card table $40,000+

◀ WORK TABLES
Work tables, such as this one made c.1810 of painted satin wood are worth. $2,500+. If American $10,000+

▲ SOFA TABLES
The best ones have two end-supports connected by a stretcher, seen here. Tables with a central pedestal base are less valuable. $2,500-5,000. American $20,000+

▲ ENGLISH PAINTED SATINWOOD
You can identify Georgian painted satinwood tables — such as this pier table made c.1775 — from those of the early 20th century by:
● the paler more mellow color of the wood
● the less colorful painted decoration. Later tables are less valuable. This one is worth about $15,000 but would cost from about $1,500 if it was 20th-century.

TABLE STYLES

Type	First made	Price/typical wood	Description
Card & Games	c.1700 Amer. 1740	$700+ mahogany, walnut, satinwood $4,000–100,000 depending on shape and carving.	Usually rectangular or demi-lune with folding top, baize-covered inside, specifically made for cards and other games
Console	c.1720 Amer. c.1750	$2,000+ giltwood	Rectangular, sometimes with serpentine front and only two front legs or carved base: made to stand against a wall
Drum	c.1800 Amer. c.1810	$1,000+ mahogany	Circular with frieze containing drawers; central pedestal support
Pembroke	c.1750 Amer. 1780s	$1,000+ mahogany, satinwood	Rectangular, serpentine or oval, with drop flaps and a drawer
Quartetto	c.1790 Amer. 1810–1815	$1,200+ mahogany, rosewood, walnut Late 19thC China Trade nests of tables $2,000+	Set of tables which fit under each other
Sofa	c.1710 Amer. 1750s	$1,000–20,000 mahogany, rosewood, satinwood $30,000–200,000+	Elongated rectangle with drop flaps and drawers
Tripod	c.1700 Amer. c.1740	$500+ mahogany Candlestand $500–30,000; tea table $1,000–500,000+	Round tilt top, tripod base usually made from solid wood

SIDEBOARDS & DINING ACCESSORIES

Once you have chosen your table and chairs, no matter what your preferred style, there's a wealth of other antique accessories available for the dining room.

Large pieces, such as serving tables and sideboards, became extremely elegant and sophisticated during the 18th century, and many are very expensive. Much more reasonable are the wealth of 19th century sideboards available; the largest are often the most affordable.

You can also find an extraordinary array of smaller dining room accessories, such as wine coolers, urns, knife boxes, cellarettes, and dumb waiters. Most were made with a very specific function in mind but can nevertheless be surprisingly versatile. These days wine coolers are more often used as containers for flowers than for wine, but they are still highly collectible.

▲ URNS
These attractivee urns are useful as well as decorative: they open up and some were fitted out to hold knives, others have spouts for iced drinking water. Pairs of Georgian urns are especially desirable. These were made c.1775 and would cost around $7,000-9,000, simpler ones $2,500-3,500; but if American, rare, $10,000+

19TH CENTURY SIDEBOARDS
Check legs haven't been altered: turned legs on 19th century sideboards are sometimes replaced with 18th century-style tapered ones to make a piece seem older – and more valuable. $2,500-4,500. American Federal side boards without gallery $5,000+ depending on amount of inlay.

◀ CELLARETTES
Most 18th century sideboards, such as this, made c.1790, have a cellarette – a deep lead-lined drawer, to hold bottles of wine for short periods before they were served.

◀ LATER
SIDEBOARDS
Provided you have
the room, you can
still find larger 19th
century sideboards in
reasonable condition
for around $250; this
one dates from c.1815,
and would be worth
$1,500–3,000.
American ones of
similar design, same
price.

HOW OLD IS IT?

This Gothic
Chippendale-style side
table might look 18th
century but in fact was
made c.1910. One tell-
tale sign is the dull flat
sheen of the wood – an
older piece would have
a mellow glowing
patina. $1,000–3,000

CELLARETTE OR WINE COOLER?

Wine coolers rarely
have lids and may
have a plug in the
base. Lidded
containers for storing
wine, such as this, are
described as
cellarettes, but the
terms overlap.
$7,000. American
classical cellarettes
with figural supports
$15,000–30,000.

▶ Wine coolers and
cellarettes can usually be
dated from their style.

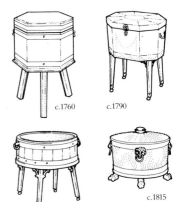

c.1760

c.1790

c.1770

c.1815

DESKS & BUREAUS

There are many different types of writing furniture, but the best known is the slant lid desk, in England called a bureau, with a hinged flap that folds up when not in use. Made in quantity from the 18th century, English desks are generally oak, walnut or mahogany, some lavishly decorated with lacquer or marquetry. They were often combined with bookcases to become desk and bookcases, or secretaries. Many are architectural in form, and were designed to co-ordinate with the design of the rooms in which they stood. Other forms of writing furniture include writing tables, kneehole desks and the curiously shaped davenport. American desks followed English styles using local woods and imported mahogany.

▼ 18TH CENTURY BUREAUS
This early 18th century bureau has many typical features which you should look for:
● small size – wider than 42in is less desirable
● attractive walnut veneers
● bun feet, although most are replacements.

Circular marks in the baseboard (below) show that a bureau originally had bun feet (even if it now has bracket feet). $3,000-7,500

LACQUER AND JAPANNING
Chinese and Japanese lacquer became popular in the 17th century, and soon English cabinet makers began to produce their own "oriental" style lacquer called Japanning, that flourished in Boston 1730-53. Black was the most common color; red is much rarer.

● Most desks are made from walnut, mahogany, or pine; the value of this one is substantial because the wood is covered with red japanning. $15,000+, American japanning is black and very rare, $20,000+.

▲ KNEEHOLE DESKS
Kneehole desks are sometimes converted from chests of drawers, so check that the drawers look complete and that veneers match.

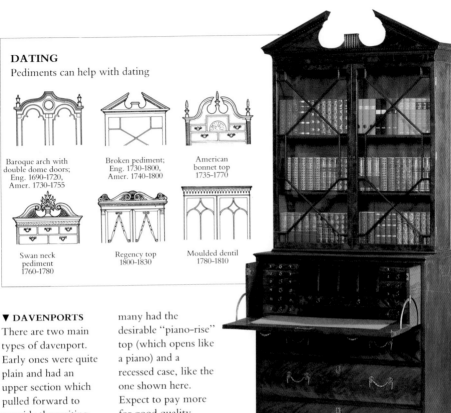

▼ DAVENPORTS
There are two main types of davenport. Early ones were quite plain and had an upper section which pulled forward to provide the writing surface. By c.1840 many had the desirable "piano-rise" top (which opens like a piano) and a recessed case, like the one shown here. Expect to pay more for good quality woods, like the burr walnut of this piece, or satinwood or rosewood. $15,000

WHAT TO LOOK FOR
Desk and bookcases:
- Bookcases should be slightly smaller than their base, but made of matching wood.

BEWARE if the base and top are flush-sided or if the top extends in back, it could be a marriage or a cut-down library bookcase.

▲ SECRETARY
When the deep top drawer of the desk and bookcase is open the front "drops" to form the writing surface. The fine quality of the interior will be reflected in the price – about $15,000 – a lesser one might be as little as $3,000.

MISCELLANEOUS FURNITURE

Antique furniture is not confined to the main types covered on the previous pages. There is also an extensive array of other interesting and attractive pieces, which, although they do not fall into any particular category, are nonetheless extremely popular with antiques collectors.

▶ MIRRORS
Don't confuse carved giltwood mirrors, such as this one, made *c.*1750, with later gilded composition ones. If instead of wood, you can see a cement-like substance over a wire frame, it's a composition mirror – and worth a fraction of the price, $5,000+. Original glass adds to value. On early glass, edges of glass uneven.

▲ OAK CHESTS
You can still find 17th century coffers for a few hundred dollars. Carving, as here, adds to value; be suspicious of stiff, regular carving – it could have been added in the 19th century. $3,500-5,000. A chest of this period is rare in America, 1670-1700, $10,000+

◀ FIRE SCREENS
17th and 18th century fire screens such as this, provided essential protection from roaring fires. According to lore they helped to stop make-up melting
They came in table models $500+ and floor models $1,000+. American 18th century fire screens $2,500-100,000 depending on design and needlework.

◀ **BEDS**
Nothing can give a more sumptuous look to a bedroom than an antique bed, but before you buy one remember they are often smaller than modern beds so you may need to have a mattress specially made. Nearly all four poster (tester) beds have been altered. Many are composites from different periods. This one has panels dating from *c.*1600 with later additions. $7,000. No beds this elaborate were made in 17th century America.

▼ **STOOLS**
Although the stool is the simplest type of seat furniture, don't expect to find them all at rock bottom prices – they can be surprisingly valuable.

This pair of French mid-18th century X-Frame stools, would be worth over $15,000+ – but you could find a Victorian or Edwardian one for much less.

▲ **COMMODES**
Originally dubbed "night tables" during the prudish Victorian era, cupboards for chamberpots were re-named "commodes". $1,000-3,000, English or American.

Pottery & Porcelain

Ceramics can be broadly divided into two main groups: pottery, which is opaque when held to the light, and porcelain, which is translucent. Within these two categories are a huge range of different types of wares which evolved over the centuries as new manufacturing techniques were developed.

If you're just beginning your collection the multitude of pottery wares produced during the 19th century could be an ideal starting point. During this period the Staffordshire area in England produced vast numbers of inexpensive household and decorative objects, which at the time cost a few shillings or less. These are still abundantly available and, although collectible, have remained relatively inexpensive.

Porcelain has long been highly prized and tends to be more expensive than pottery. The field is divided into two main groups, hard- and soft-paste porcelain. Many pieces have marks of some type but these are no guarantee of authenticity because many factories copied each other's marks to make their products more desirable.

Value is usually a matter of size, age, rarity, decorative appeal and, above all, condition. European 18th century porcelain tends to be very high priced but you can often buy damaged pieces for a fraction of the cost of those in perfect condition.

BASICS

When you first look at a piece of pottery or porcelain, an understanding of the materials and techniques used in its manufacture can help you identify its origin, date and how much it might be worth. The three main factors to assess are:
- Material
- Glaze
- Decoration

MATERIALS
Pottery
This has a relatively coarse texture, compared with porcelain, and is usually opaque if held to the light; the two main types are earthenware, and non-porous stoneware.

Earthenware
Clay fired at a temperature of less than 2200F (1200C) is classified as earthenware. The body is porous, and may be white, buff, brown, red or grey, depending on the color of the clay and its iron content.

Stoneware
This is made from clay which can withstand firing at a temperature of up to 2250F (1400C). The high firing temperature makes the clay fuse into the non-porous body which does not absorb liquids, and may be semi-translucent. Bodies vary in color.

Porcelain
If it's slightly translucent the chances are it's porcelain; now you must decide which type — hard- or soft-paste. If the body looks smooth, like icing sugar, it is probably hard-paste, if it looks granular, like sand, it is more likely to be soft-paste.

Hard-paste porcelain

A hard-paste porcelain Meissen quatrefoil dish $2,000-3,000

All Chinese and much Continental porcelain is hard-paste, made from kaolin (china clay) and petuntse (china stone). First the object is fired, then dipped in glaze, then refired. The china stone bonds the particles of clay together and gives translucency. Because the firing takes place at a very high temperature the object attains the consistency of glass.

The first hard-paste porcelain was made in China in the 9th century AD. In Europe the Meissen factory began producing porcelain in the early 18th century, and before long, factories throughout Europe began making hard-paste porcelain.

Soft-paste porcelain

A Chelsea soft-paste porcelain group depicting Winter and Spring $2,000–3,000

As the name suggests, soft-paste porcelain is more vulnerable to scratching than hard-paste. There are several types of soft-paste porcelain, each using fine clay combined with different ingredients to give translucency.

Soft-paste can often be identified because the glaze sits on the surface, and feels warmer and softer to the touch and looks less glittering in appearance than hard-paste. Chips in soft-paste look floury, like fine pastry; in hard-paste porcelain chips look glassy.

Soft-paste porcelain was first produced in Italy during the 16th century. Later factories using soft-paste include St Cloud, Chantilly, Vincennes, Sèvres, Capodimonte and Chelsea.

Bone China
This is a type of English porcelain first made c.1794 using a large proportion of bone-ash added to hard-paste ingredients. This body was used by prominent English factories such as Spode, Flight & Barr, Derby, Rockingham, Coalport and Minton.

GLAZES
Glazes can be translucent, opaque, or colored. Hard-paste porcelain was given a feldspar glaze, which fused with the body when fired. On soft-paste porcelain the glaze tends to pool in the crevices.

A variety of different glazes were used on pottery and porcelain, the main ones are:

Lead glaze
Used on most soft-paste porcelain, and on earthenwares such as creamware.

A Dutch Delftware tin glaze tortoise $2,000–3,000

Tin glaze
A glaze to which tin oxide has been added to give an opaque white finish.

Salt glaze
A glaze formed by throwing common salt into the kiln at about 1800F (1000C) during the firing.

DECORATIVE TECHNIQUES
Decoration can be added before or after glazing. Underglaze decoration means the colors have been added before glazing.

Underglaze blue
Blue pigment, made of cobalt, was used on Chinese blue and white porcelain, European delftware, and soft-paste porcelain.

Overglaze enamels
Overglaze enamels were made by adding metallic oxide to molten glass and reducing the cooled mixture, which, when combined with an oily medium, could be painted over the glaze and fused to it by firing. The range of colors was larger than underglaze colors.

MARKS
Marks are found on the base of many objects. These may include factory marks, which changed periodically and can therefore help with dating, and maker's initials.
● Many marks were copied or faked so marks should not be taken as a guarantee of authenticity.

CHINESE POTTERY & PORCELAIN

Mention Chinese ceramics and many people immediately think of priceless Ming and assume that this collecting area is definitely beyond their reach. In fact, because fine pottery and porcelain have been produced in China for longer than anywhere else in the world, it's not hard to find pieces that are both decorative and inexpensive – although there are of course some extremely high priced objects as well.

The Chinese discovered the art of making porcelain, in the Tang Dynasty, AD618-906. When Dutch traders began importing Chinese porcelain to Europe in the 17th century (the late Ming period) no European maker had yet been able to produce such fine quality wares and there was a huge demand for Chinese porcelain – as well as a scramble to find out how it was made (see p62). Nearly all porcelain was blue and white until *c.*1700, when more varied color schemes such as *famille rose* and *famille verte* were introduced. The many objects made for the European market, often using Western shapes decorated with traditional Chinese designs, are known as "export wares".

Later Chinese Dynasties			
Wei	386–557	Liao	907–1125
Sui	589–617	Sung	960–1280
Tang	618–906	Chin	1115–1260
5 Dyn-		Yuan	1280–1368
asties	907–960	Ming	1368–1644
		Qing	1644–1916

MING

VALUE DEPENDS ON QUALITY AND CONDITION. PROVINCIAL EXPORT PIECES OF LESSER QUALITY, OR SLIGHTLY CHIPPED OR CRACKED WARES, CAN BE SURPRISINGLY AFFORDABLE. THIS BOWL WOULD BE WORTH OVER $200,000 BUT YOU CAN FIND IMPERIAL PIECES WITH HAIRLINE CRACKS FOR FAR LESS, $10,000

BEWARE
Don't rely on dynasty reign marks alone for dating Chinese porcelain – as many as 80% are not of the period, and were simply used to show respect for earlier classical wares.

MING OR QING?
Ming patterns were often repeated during the Qing period; Ming pieces can be identified by:
● thick bluish glaze, suffused with bubbles
● tendency to reddish oxidization
● knife marks on the high footrim.

SYMBOLS

The decoration on Chinese ceramics usually has symbolic significance:

Dragons represent authority, strength, wisdom, and the Emperor.

Pairs of ducks symbolize marital bliss.

The peony shows love, beauty, happiness and honor.

The pine, *prunus* and bamboo together denote spiritual harmony.

Cranes show longevity, and transport for Immortals.

▲ BLUE AND WHITE

Chinese blue and white was made by painting the blue decoration on the porcelain before glazing – so it is known as underglaze blue. Later wares, such as these Qing export vases are part of a five-piece garniture. Even though the central vase is missing a cover it is worth $2,000-3,000. Later wares have more complicated designs, more evenly applied, thinner glaze.

▲ FAMILLE VERTE

Famille verte ("green family") porcelain is dominated by a brilliant green and was used to decorate export wares from the Kangxi period (1662-1722). Price if 16in $5,500-25,000 depending on quality.

▲ FAMILLE ROSE

Opaque pink enamel decorated wares are termed *"famille rose"* ("pink family"). Often copied in the 19th century by the French maker Samson, crackling in the enamel colors (a fine net-work of cracks) is a good sign the piece is authentic. 8in plate $600-800

JAPANESE POTTERY & PORCELAIN

Japanese ceramics have long been among the most sought after of all Oriental works of art. Although their wares often reflect the influence of Chinese styles, Japanese potters developed their own distinctive color schemes and patterns. According to legend, the first Japanese porcelain was made in 1616, in the town of Arita, some years after it was first made in nearby China. The wares you are most likely to come across are Arita, Imari, Kakiemon and Satsuma. Not all of these cost a fortune – you can still find pieces for a few hundred dollars or less. Decoration can affect value dramatically. The plate below is worth over $15,000 because it is decorated with the cipher of the Dutch East Indian Company. Without this it would be worth $4,000-5,000.

JAPANESE OR CHINESE?

Japanese blue and white wares, such as this *c.*1690 Arita export dish copy Chinese prototypes. Distinctive Japanese features are:

- granular porcelain
- extremely dark (as here) or soft underglaze blue
- three or more spur marks, on the underside. $12,000+

◀ **ARITA WARES**
Arita porcelain is called after the town of Arita, where Japanese porcelain production was concentrated. Arita, Imari and Kakiemon ware were all made in the same area but Arita is the more inclusive term and is used to describe more than just blue and white wares.

▶ **SATSUMA WARE**
Satsuma is recognizable by its cream colored crackle-glaze ground, and lavish gold decoration. It was made during the Meiji period 1867-1912. Prices vary: high quality pieces can bring $10,000+ but you can find quickly-painted pieces for as little as $150. This late 19th century vase is one of a signed pair worth about $5,000

▲ **KAKIEMON**
Named after the family said to have developed fine white porcelain and a distinctive style of enamelling in Japan. You can identify

Kakeimon wares such as this dish by the white ground, asymmetrical high quality polychrome decoration. Large plate $12,000-15,000; small under $5,000.

IMARI

OF ALL THE TYPES OF
JAPANESE CERAMICS,
IMARI (NAMED AFTER
THE PORT THROUGH
WHICH THEY WERE
SHIPPED TO EUROPE)
ARE THE ONES YOU
SEE MOST
FREQUENTLY. THIS
LATE 17TH CENTURY
VASE HAS MANY OF
THE FEATURES
CHARACTERISTIC OF
IMARI WARES. $7,000–
10,000 FOR THIS LARGE
VASE.

REMEMBER . . .

Remove loose lids from jars
before you pick them up to
examine them.

MANUFACTURE

Imari pieces were
usually painted with
dark underglaze blue
decoration (see p63),
glazed, fired,
enamelled with colors
and fired again.

DECORATION

Floral designs or
landscapes are usually
set in shaped reserves
set off by underglaze
blue. Some pieces
have figural knobs.

COLORS

Colors typical of
Imari are dark blue,
iron-red, green and
aubergine. It was
often gilded for the
Western taste.
The touches of green
on this vase indicate
its high quality.

CONDITION

Condition is crucial
to value. However,
damage can usually
be restored and
buying a damaged
piece can be an
affordable starting
point if you're on a
limited budget.

TYPES

Large display wares
such as this vase,
which is designed to
stand on a
mantelpiece, are
keenly sought after;
pairs and sets (called
garnitures) always
command a premium.

FAKES AND COPIES

Imari has been faked
and imitated.
18th and 19th century
copies are valuable
in their own right.
Modern copies, such as
this Korean vase, may
be expensive but have
little status as
collectibles.

EARLY ENGLISH POTTERY

Love it or hate it – the naïvety of early English pottery leaves few indifferent to its charms and there are enough smitten collectors to make many of the rarest pieces extremely valuable. During the late 17th and early 18th centuries English pottery underwent a period of rapid development and an enormously varied range of new wares and decorative techniques was developed. Pottery is categorized by the type of body from

SLIPWARE	ENGLISH DELFT	SALTGLAZE STONEWARE
*c.*1720 SLIPWARE BAKING DISH $14,000+	*c.*1730 BLUE DASH CHARGER $15,000+	18thC TWO-HANDLED CUP $2,500–3,000
HOW, WHEN & WHERE Made from red or buff earthenware, decorated with white or colored slip (diluted clay). Zig-zag, feathered and marble designs predominate. Produced in Staffordshire, Wrotham Kent, Bideford, Barnstaple, Wales, Wiltshire, Sussex. Dates from 17th-mid-18th century.	Made from earthenware with a white tin glaze, in Southwark, Lambeth, Bristol and Liverpool. Naïve designs of figures, animals and floral subjects mainly painted in blue, yellow, green and manganese. Known as "delftware" from Georgian times. Dates from mid 16th-late 18thC.	White Devon clay and powdered flint added to earthenware made light weight white wares; salt thrown in kiln during firing formed glaze pitted like an orange skin. After *c.*1745 more use of *famille rose* type enamel colors to imitate Chinese porcelain. Made in Staffordshire, from mid-18thC.
WHAT TO LOOK FOR Dishes and mugs. Named or dated wares, especially those by best-known maker Thomas Toft, who occasionally signed his wares on the front – no marks usually. Beware of skillful fakes.	Blue-dash chargers – (plates with blue strokes around edge as in the illustration; often decorated with monarchs); barbers' bowls, pill slabs, flower bricks. Seldom marked. Chips are acceptable.	Figures and pew groups (very rare), loving cups, mugs, plates, jugs formed as owls, unusually shaped teapots (camels, houses) are usually unmarked.

which it is made (such as earthenware, stone ware, creamware) and the type of glaze used (such as tin glaze, salt glaze). If you are thinking of collecting early pottery it's a good idea to learn the differences between some of the most important categories. Below are six types of pottery made before c.1770 (for post 1770 see p78), as well as pointers on what pieces you can expect to see and which are most sought after.

WHIELDON	AGATEWARE	CREAMWARE	
WHIELDON MID-18thC PUG $3,500	c.1745 AGATEWARE CAT WITH MOUSE $3,000	c.1760 CREAMWARE TEAPOT, $2,500+	
Mid-18thC Staffordshire potter, Thomas Whieldon, developed lead glazed pottery for tablewares and figures, incorporating metallic oxides in shades of green, brown, grey, blue and yellow.	Layers of differently colored clays wedged together, sliced to build up mingled layers resembling agate was molded into wares. Lead and salt glaze variously used; made in Staffordshire in 18thC.	Cream-colored earthenware with transparent lead glaze, developed by Wedgwood in 1760s, also made in other Staffordshire potteries and in Leeds, Bristol, Liverpool, Swansea and Derby. May be enamelled, transfer printed or pierced.	HOW, WHEN & WHERE
Well-modeled animals like this dog; unusually shaped wares, candlestick figures, cow creamers, cottages with figures. Table wares are less expensive. Never marked.	Cats, as shown, tewares, jugs, coffee and chocolate pots, shell shaped wares – inspired by contemporary silver; pieces with more than two differently colored clays. Never marked.	Red and black enamelling by Robinson & Rhodes; wares marked "Wedgwood"; pierced wares which may be marked "Leeds Pottery". Molded pieces such as cruets and centrepieces. Few creamwares are marked.	WHAT TO LOOK FOR

CONTINENTAL POTTERY

Most Continental pottery is earthenware covered with a tin oxide glaze. Tin-glazed earthenware is given different names in various countries. In Italy and Spain it is called *maiolica*, in France and Germany *faïence*, and in the Netherlands Delft, after the town in Holland where it was made.

The richly colored designs and motifs of Continental pottery of the 17th and 18th centuries provided a popular source of inspiration for makers in the 19th century and later. Most of these later copies are highly decorative and collectible in their own right.

▶ **SPANISH MAIOLICA**
Shiny metallic lustre decoration, as on this rare 15th century dish, is characteristic of Spanish pottery. Similar pieces were reproduced in Italy in the late 19th century by the Cantagalli factory – these copies were originally marked with a singing cockerel on the base. $10,000–15,000

▲ **DRUG JARS**
Maiolica apothecaries' drug jars were made both for display and for storage – hence their colorful decoration. Shapes vary according to the jar's original contents. Wet drugs were stored in bulbous jars with spouts like this, dry drugs were usually stored in cylindrical ones. $10,000–15,000

▲ **FRENCH FAÏENCE**
This well-painted 18th century plate was made by one of the most prominent French factories – that of the Veuve (widow) Perrin. Many wares from this factory are marked "VP", but the mark is also seen on copies, so don't rely on the mark alone and always check the quality of the painting. $1,000–1,500

◀ **DUTCH DELFT**
Tulips were a Dutch obsession and Delft tulip vases were made in simple cushion shapes like this. Others resembled elaborate pagodas, standing several feet tall. $6,000–8,000

BEWARE

Some genuine pieces of *maiolica*, *faïence* and Delft have fake inscriptions to make them seem more valuable: be suspicious if the calligraphy seems to lack fluidity and if you see any grey specks in unglazed areas – a sign the piece has been refired.

COPIES

Many honest copies were made in the 19th century, marked by makers such as Doccia, Molaroni, Maiolica Artistica Pesarese and Bruno Buratti – these are collectible but considerably less valuable.

CONDITION

Don't expect to find early *maiolica* in perfect condition, chips and cracks are commonplace and pieces are still valuable despite damage. The rim of this tazza is replaced in part but it is still worth over $12,000, less than a third as much as a perfect one, because the painting is of such high quality. You can find smaller, less finely painted pieces from about $750.

ITALIAN *MAIOLICA*

THE SURFACE OF VALUABLE *ISTORIATO* (STORY) DISHES, SUCH AS THIS 16TH CENTURY URBINO TAZZA, ARE USED LIKE THE CANVAS OF A PAINTING TO SHOW A MYTHOLOGICAL OR RELIGIOUS SUBJECT – THIS PICTURE OF REBECCA AND ISAAC IS TAKEN FROM A RAPHAEL DRAWING.

COLORS

As in most Italian *maiolica*, the colors that predominate are blue, yellow, orange, black and green. If a wider range of colors is used it may indicate the piece is of higher quality.

CONTINENTAL PORCELAIN FIGURES

Ask anyone to name a European porcelain factory and the chances are the first one they'll think of will be Meissen. This factory is famous because it was the first in Europe to discover the secret of making hard-paste porcelain (in the early 18th century) and because of the exceptionally high quality of its products.

Meissen began to concentrate on producing figures from *c*.1730, following the arrival of a young sculptor named Johann Joachim Kandler. Before long, Kandler's figures became even more popular than Meissen tablewares. As other porcelain factories sprang up throughout Europe, they too began producing figures in the style of Meissen – some of them even using the Meissen crossed swords mark to make their pieces more tempting.

If you're a new collector you may find the differences between the figures made by the various factories are often so small as to be easily overlooked. But as you become more experienced, details such as the modelling, the shape of a base, the colors and the glaze can tell you by whom and when a piece was made. Don't be afraid to pick up the figures and look underneath for marks – but remember to support them well in your hand when you do!

◀ MEISSEN
You may think this twisting figure of a piper, made *c*.1740, looks as if it's about to topple over – but the turning pose is typical of the best Meissen figures which are always full of movement. $18,000-20,000

REMEMBER . . .
Crossed swords alone don't mean you have a piece of Meissen – this is the most commonly faked mark and was copied by Worcester, Minton, Bow and Derby – among others!

▶ VIENNA
The different colors on a figure can tell you where it was made. The combination of strong green, pale mauve, puce, and yellow on this group is typical of many *c*.1760-70 Vienna figures. $4,500-6,000

▲ FRANKENTHAL
Frankenthal figures, such as this, are often of high quality despite their rather stiff poses. Features typical of Frankenthal are:
● large hands
● doll-like faces
● arched edge to bases
● tufts of green moss.
$1,500-2,500

IS IT MEISSEN?

Is the figure made from white paste, perhaps with a slight grey tinge? —NO→ ● If it is slightly blue and smoky it might be made by Vienna. → ● If it has a distinct grey tone it may be modern Meissen.

↓YES

Is it obviously separately modelled from the base? —NO→ ● If it looks as if it is growing out of its base it could be by Nymphenburg. → A *c*.1760 Nymphenburg figure of Summer

↓YES

Is the base covered with flowers and leaves? —NO→ ● If it has patches of moss it could be Frankenthal
● If it has a rough base or triangular gilt patterns it might be Vienna. → ● If it has an undulating base with gilt or puce scrolls it might be Frankenthal.

↓YES

Is the face severely modelled but subtly colored? —NO→ ● If the features are very childlike it could be by Hochst.

A Hochst group *c*.1770 $4,000–6,000

↓YES

Is the painting very detailed, using either bold or pastel shades? —NO→ ● The colors on 19thC Meissen are often washed out and lack the fine details of the best 18thC pieces.

↓YES

Is it marked with crossed swords on the base, back or on the side? —NO→ ● If there is no mark it could be an early figure by Vienna.

MARKS OF OTHER MAKERS

▲ Hochst, ◀ Frankenthal, Nymphenburg

IF ALL THE ANSWERS ARE YES, YOU MAY HAVE A PIECE OF MEISSEN.

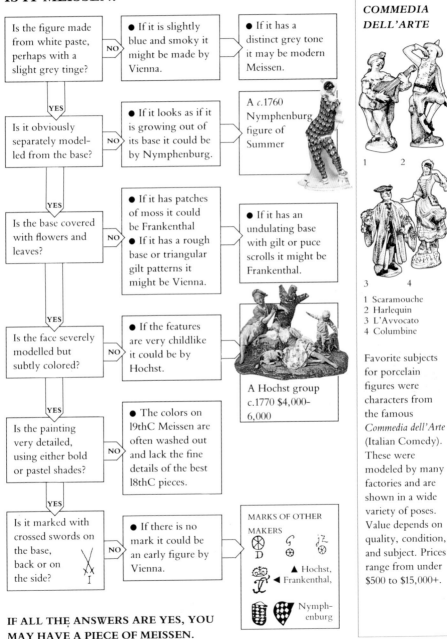

COMMEDIA DELL'ARTE

1 Scaramouche
2 Harlequin
3 L'Avvocato
4 Columbine

Favorite subjects for porcelain figures were characters from the famous *Commedia dell'Arte* (Italian Comedy). These were modeled by many factories and are shown in a wide variety of poses. Value depends on quality, condition, and subject. Prices range from under $500 to $15,000+.

CONTINENTAL TABLEWARES

There are various ways you can form an interesting and attractive collection of Continental porcelain. You might decide to concentrate on the wares of one particular factory, or a particular type of ware, say coffee cups, which can still be bought singly and affordably. Alternatively, you may want to concentrate on pieces with a common style of decoration, perhaps painted with landscapes or flowers.

Whatever you choose, you will find Continental porcelain in a huge range of styles, shapes, colors – and prices. Value is largely a matter of four key factors: maker or factory, style, quality and condition. Identification is usually a matter of recognizing the characteristic features of each factory's wares such as the shapes, colors and type of paste and glaze they used. It is the combination of these factors, together with the mark (if there is one), which can tell you whether a piece is genuine or not.

▶ **CONDITION**
All these unusual Meissen vegetables have had some restoration, and this has reduced their value (to about $900 for the artichoke or the pair of peas). In perfect condition they would be worth about twice as much.

▲ **DECORATION**
Decoration can give away the maker's identity – Middle

Eastern figures, as seen on this plate, are typical of the Paris factory. $1,500-2,000

▶ **STYLES**
Dating can be confusing because during the 19th century earlier styles were often repeated. This Sèvres tea-service uses shapes fashionable in c.1790, but in fact was made in 1837. $6,000-8,000

COPIES

Some copies are very skilful and are collectible in their own right. One of the most famous 19th century copyists, Edmé Samson of Paris, made this copy (left) of a Meissen original (right). You can tell it's a copy by the greyish color of the porcelain, the heavier weight, and less lavish gilding. Copy $400–600; original $8,000-12,000.

BEWARE

It's a great mistake to attach too much importance to marks, because many were copied – more than 90% of the Vincennes/early Sèvres linked Ls appear on later copies. One way of detecting fakes is by looking at the paste from which the piece is made – most copies are on hard-paste, but the original mark was used only for soft-paste (see p62 for how to tell the difference).

(see p62 for how to tell the difference)

▶ SÈVRES

This Sèvres jug can be dated by the distinctive pink known as *"Rose Pompadour"* (after King Louis XV's mistress, Madame Pompadour). This color was introduced c.1757 and probably discontinued after Madame Pompadour's death in 1764. $4,000–6,000+

COLORS

Certain colors are associated with particular factories or periods. Some rare colors increase value.
1 Greyish turquoise: Meissen, c.1770
2 *Bleu Celeste,* Sèvres
3 Apple Green, Sèvres
4 Böttger Green, early Meissen
5 Lemon yellow, Meissen c.1730-50
6 Egg Yolk, Meissen c.1730-40
7 Tan, German and Swiss factories
8 Russet, Fürstenberg, Ludwigsburg
9 Dark Brown, German factories
10 Iron red, all factories
11 Purple, Meissen
12 Claret, Vienna
13 Puce, German factories, mid-18thC
14 *Rose Pompadour,* Sèvres 1760s
15 Lilac, Meissen, 1740-55

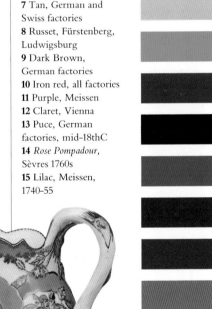

EARLY ENGLISH PORCELAIN

Compared with lavishly decorated Continental wares, early English porcelain may seem relatively unsophisticated – but to many collectors this simplicity is fundamental to its appeal.

English makers tended to be much slower than their Continental counterparts in discovering how to make porcelain. One of the first English porcelain factories – Chelsea – was established by a French silversmith, Nicholas Sprimont in 1745, nearly half a century after porcelain had first been made in Germany and France. Wares made by Chelsea were mainly intended for the luxury end of the market and are among the most sought-after of all English porcelain.

Among the other famous names which became established soon after are Bow, Worcester and Derby. The best way of learning how to recognize the wares of different factories is to study and handle as much porcelain as possible. This way you will become familiar with the styles, colors, glazes and shapes used. As with almost any type of porcelain, marks are often spurious – they can be a help but should never be solely relied upon.

▲ BOW
Bow, the largest English porcelain factory in the mid-18th century, specialized in Oriental-style wares, such as this tureen, which has three features typical of most Bow pieces:
● white chalky paste
● greenish glassy glaze
● heavy potting.
$2,000–3,000

◄ DERBY
English figures are usually more primitively modelled than those made on the Continent and tend to be less expensive. This Derby figure is worth $1,200–1,800

MARKS

Bow Marks   Derby Marks   Worcester Marks

LOOKING AT PORCELAIN

Never pick a piece of porcelain up by the handle – it might come off. Support the main body firmly with both hands.

▶ WORCESTER
Hold a piece of Worcester up to the light and you should see a greenish tinge, perhaps with small patches of pinpricks. The molded cabbage-leaf decoration on this jug is typical of Worcester. $1,500–2,500+

The shadows given to the insects are a device copied from Meissen and make them stand out more dramatically.

A typical feature of Chelsea is the way the insects are painted on a larger scale than the flowers.

Chelsea wares can be distinguished from most other botanical plates because the flowers take up almost the entire surface of the plate.

CHELSEA

CHELSEA BOTANICAL PLATES OF THE 1750S ARE CALLED "HANS SLOANE" WARES BECAUSE THE DESIGNS WERE BASED ON PRINTS OF FLOWERS FROM SIR HANS SLOANE'S CHELSEA PHYSIC GARDEN.

CHELSEA MARKS

Chelsea wares are divided into groups according to the four marks used during the life of the factory. This plate, marked with a red anchor, dates from c.1752-57.

	Triangle period	1745–49
	Raised anchor period	1749–52
	Red anchor period	1752–57
	Gold anchor period	1759–69

Despite a small crack, the high quality painting makes this one of the most valuable type of botanical plate, worth $4,000–5,000; if perfect $8,000–12,000

BEWARE
Fake red and gold anchor marks are usually much larger than the genuine ones.

LATER ENGLISH POTTERY

Not only is the pottery of the 19th century colorful and decorative, it can often provide you with a fascinating visual record of the major events and personalities of the Victorian age. Firms such as Pratt & Co. perfected color transfer printing from *c*.1840 and pot lids, boxes, plates and other wares were decorated with images of the Royal family, the Crimean War and the Great Exhibition. Royal events such as Queen Victoria's wedding, coronation and jubilees inspired huge numbers of specially decorated wares. Originally sold for a few shillings, many are now avidly sought after. Other highly popular collectibles include Staffordshire figures, blue and white transfer printed wares, Wemyss-ware and ironstone. If all these are too expensive, look out for 19th century tiles – you can find Victorian printed versions at affordable prices.

▲ PRINTED BLUE AND WHITE POTTERY
Value depends on condition and pattern: because these three meat platters are all slightly damaged, they are moderately priced, between $65-150 each. Less sought-after patterns start at around $100. With rare American views $1,000-10,000+.

◀ WEDGWOOD
Some colored objects, such as this 1780s "Jasperware" vase, were made by dipping the object into slip (diluted clay). These wares were made throughout the 19th century and later. The blue used in the 19th century tends to be darker; 20th century copies are of lesser quality. $1,500-2,000

▲ DINNER SERVICES
This Mason's Ironstone dinner service is made of heavy earthenware first patented in 1813. It's usually easy to identify wares made by this factory as they're nearly always marked. If the word "Improved" appears on the factory mark it means the piece was made after *c*.1840.

● Large dinner services are especially valuable. $5,000-7,000+ for 30 or 40 pieces.

WEMYSS WARE

Wemyss pigs such as this were made in Fife, Scotland, from 1880. There is also a wide range of Wemyss mugs, vases, jugs and jam pots, all of which have risen in value dramatically. This pig is probably worth more than $400.

WHAT TO LOOK FOR

- good quality painting
- tablewares with red borders – these are early
- figurative subjects – cockerels, cats, bees and pigs
- large pieces.

STAFFORDSHIRE FIGURES

COLORFUL POTTERY FIGURES, SUCH AS THIS SPANIEL, WERE PRODUCED IN QUANTITY THROUGHOUT THE 19TH CENTURY. SOME WERE MADE IN SCOTLAND AND WALES BUT MOST CAME FROM THE STAFFORDSHIRE POTTERIES, SO ALL FIGURES OF THIS TYPE ARE KNOWN AS STAFFORDSHIRE FIGURES; NEARLY ALL OF THEM ARE UNMARKED.

PAINTING

The detailed painting of the dog's face is a sign of quality and indicates an early date – later figures are more simply painted.

VALUE

Subject matter and rarity affect the price – animals and royal, political and military subjects are particularly desirable. The spaniel would be worth around $800-1,200.

REPRODUCTION OR FAKE?

Less valuable Staffordshire figures, reproduced throughout the 20th century, often from the same molds as genuine Victorian pieces, can be identified in several key ways:

Genuine	Copy or Fake
● crisp modeling	● soft definition
● detailed painting	● little detail
● colorful decoration	● weak color
● finger marks inside – from press molding	● smooth inside – from slip casting
● thick walls	● thin fragile walls
● erratic, wide spaced crackling in glaze	● regular, exaggerated crackling in glaze
● soft gilding	● bright gilding
● kiln grit and glaze on foot	● glaze wiped from foot

19TH CENTURY ENGLISH PORCELAIN

Various exciting new porcelain-making techniques were introduced and perfected in the 19th century. The development of bone china, which was made from the same ingredients as hard-paste porcelain (see p63) with large quantities of animal bone added, meant that less expensive porcelain became widely available.

Practical, relatively inexpensive dinner, dessert and tea services were made in large quantities, many of them embellished with printed decoration, which was also developed at this period.

You can still buy simple transfer-printed flat wares and hollow wares quite inexpensively. Some of the most affordable collectibles are those made by the Goss factory from the second half of the 19th century. Their statuettes and ornaments with printed decoration are available for under $75.

BEWARE

Don't confuse hand painting, which increases value, with a hand-enamelled print (as seen on the left), which is generally less desirable. If it's hand-enamelled you'll be able to see the print underneath the enamel.

▲ PRINTED CHINA

Although hand-painted wares are usually more desirable than those with transfer printed decoration, there are some exceptions. This teapot shows Queen Victoria and Prince Albert – a royal subject always pushes up the price and this would be worth $300-500.

◀ ROCKINGHAM

You may think this is a strange teapot but in fact it's a violeteer – a pot to hold petals and herbs. The highly elaborate molded and flower encrusted decoration is typical of this factory. $800-1,200

◀ SPODE

Spode was one of the first factories to use bone china. You can recognize earlier (pre-1830) pieces by their mark, which was usually hand painted – later it was printed. Features typical of Spode porcelain are:
● pattern number in red
● very thin potting
● thin smooth white glaze.
  $1,500-2,500

At the other end of the spectrum, important factories such as Rockingham, Spode and Minton made a variety of highly ornamental wares, often using lavish gilding, elaborate high relief floral decorations and new techniques such as *pâte-sur-pâte*. Value is usually a matter of decorative appeal. Expect to pay more for hand-painted decoration. Any elaborately decorated piece will usually command a premium.

HOW TO DATE 19TH AND 20TH CENTURY PORCELAIN	
"Royal" in trademark	after 1850
"Limited" or "Ltd" after name	after 1860
"Trade Mark"	after *c.*1870
"England" in trademark	after 1890
"Bone China"	20th century
"Made in England"	20th century

▼ MINTON
One of the innovations introduced by Minton during the 19th century was the technique of *pâte-sur-pâte*. This involved applying layers of white slip (a mixture of clay and water) to a dark body which was then hand carved to expose the dark ground. The process was a laborious one and pieces were always expensive; this *pâte-sur-pâte* vase would be worth $3,000–4,500.

◀ COALPORT
French designs of the 18th century became popular again in the 19th century. Coalport was one of the most famous factories to produce porcelain in the style of Sèvres. This vase is particularly desirable because of its high quality hand-painted birds. $800–1,200+
● Coalport is often marked AD 1750. This is the date the company was founded, not the date of production.

▶ PARIAN
Although this elegant figure looks as if it's carved from marble, it's actually made from Parian, a type of porcelain. Parian figures became popular in the mid-19th century; the best were made (and marked) by factories such as Worcester (as this one is), Copeland, Belleek or Wedgwood and are very detailed. Unmarked figures are much less valuable. $800

From the earliest times silversmiths realized that pure silver was unworkably soft, and had to be mixed with other more resilient base metals before it could be made into objects.

A silver standard was introduced in Britain in 1300 and all silver objects made after this date had to be tested, and marked to show they contained more than 92.5% pure silver. This marking system has survived in Britain and Ireland with few modifications to the present day. Marks provide the collector of English silver with an invaluable aid. You may come across silver with fake or altered marks, or unmarked pieces, but these are relatively scarce, and once you have learned to "read" the marks, you will be able to identify where, when, and (often) who made most pieces of silver. Nonetheless, always make sure the style is consistent with the date of the marks. Although most pieces of American silver are marked with the initials or name of the maker, there was no official system of hallmarking. Continental silver is also usually marked by the maker. Despite the vagaries of fashion, old silver has remained one of the most enduring and popular collecting areas. Small 19th century objects, old Sheffield plate and electroplate all offer excellent value.

BASICS

HALLMARKS

There are four main English marks:
- The sterling guarantee
- The town mark
- The date letter
- The maker's mark

Sterling guarantee mark

1 Leopard's head
2 Leopard's head crowned
3 Lion *passant*

Silver that is at least 92.5% pure is termed "sterling" silver. All silver objects of sterling quality were stamped with a leopard's head from 1300. By 1458 the leopard had a crown; from 1544 the sterling mark changed to a lion *passant*, shown walking to the left (after this date the leopard's head was used as the London town mark).

4 Britannia mark
5 Lion's head

Between 1697 and 1720, a higher standard of silver, known as the Britannia standard, was introduced. During this period the sterling mark was replaced by a figure of Britannia, and a lion's head in profile.

Town marks

Marks showing where a piece was assayed were introduced *c.*1600. Some of the commonest are:

6   7   8

9   10   11

12   13   14

6 London
7 Birmingham
8 Chester
9 Dublin
10 Exeter
11 Edinburgh
12 Glasgow
13 Sheffield
14 York

Date letters

15 16 17 18

15 1721   17 1781
16 1741   18 1801

Marking with a date letter, which changed each year, was introduced in the 15th century in London, and later in other parts of the country. The letters usually follow an alphabetical sequence, but are unique to each assay office. The letter is contained within a shield.

Maker's mark

19 Matthew Boulton
20 John Cafe
21 Robert Hennell
22 Paul Storr

Marks to show the identity of the maker were used from the 14th century. The earliest were pictorial symbols, but from the late 17th century marks increasingly incorporated the silversmith's initials.

ALTERED AND FAKE MARKS
Forged marks
Fake marks are usually less clearly defined than genuine ones; if they have been made by recasting a genuine piece there may be small granulations visible in the outline.

Transposed marks
Marks are sometimes taken from a low value object and inserted in a larger,

potentially more valuable one. If you breathe on transposed marks you should be able to see a faint outline around the marks where they were soldered in.

Illegal Alterations
An Act of 1844 made it illegal to alter any piece of silver without hallmarking the additions. However, many pieces were updated to make them more useful, or more fashionable, rather than to deliberately deceive.

PATINA
Over years of use, silver develops a soft glow, or patina, caused by accumulated scratching and knocks and bruises. This patina is important to value. Repolishing old silver on a buffing wheel can destroy the patina of a piece and is usually undesirable.

WEIGHT
Although an item which is heavier than average may not appear larger or heavier, extra weight is usually synonymous with quality, and heavier

pieces tend to be more valuable.

STYLES AND DECORATION
Silver styles reflect the taste of the period, and can often provide a good indication of date. Decoration may be applied to the surface or the border of a piece and usually adds to value (see p93 for some of the different types found).

CONDITION
Repairs are usually detrimental to value. If lead has been used in the repair it can be especially unsightly. Areas particularly vulnerable to damage are:
- **Feet:** these can be pushed up through the base.
- **Handles:** the metal of the body may be pulled away by the handle.
- **Hinges:** can be broken and are often difficult to repair.
- **Pierced decoration:** may be relatively fragile and prone to damage.

SHEFFIELD PLATE
Sheffield plate, made from a fusion of

copper and silver, was introduced c.1740. Most Sheffield plate is unmarked, although some early 19th century pieces had marks very similar to those found on silver.
- A piece with "Sheffield plate" stamped on it is electroplate made in Sheffield in the 19th century, not genuine Sheffield plate.
- Sheffield plate tends to be much less expensive than silver, but the best pieces are eagerly collected.

ELECTROPLATE
This method, involving covering a base metal with a thin layer of silver by electro-deposition, was used from c.1840. The base metal was initially copper, but later nickel was used, hence the term EPNS (electro-plated nickel silver). Electroplate is usually marked by its maker, or bears indications of quality.
- Apart from pieces by an eminent maker such as Elkington, electroplate is less collectible than other types of silver.

TEAPOTS, CHOCOLATE POTS &

Tea, coffee and chocolate became fashionable in the late 17th century, and over the next two centuries large numbers of pots for serving these drinks were made.

The shapes of tea and coffee pots can help with dating them, but because many 18th century styles were repeated in the 19th and 20th centuries you need to check the marks on the base to tell whether the piece is a later reproduction. There is nothing wrong with buying, say, a 19th century coffee pot in an 18th century style, provided the marks are correct for the date it was made and the pot is priced accordingly. Bear in mind that coffee and teapots were made to be used and may have become well worn as a result – before you buy one examine it carefully for damage, which can be expensive to repair.

MARKING
Teapots are usually marked on the base – it's less common to find marks on the side. The maker's mark on a handle may be different from that on the body, as handles are nearly always later replacements. Lids should also be marked.

▲ TEAPOTS
The "bullet" teapot has a lid with a concealed hinge, which was attached before the base was soldered on. Check lids carefully before buying – if the hinge is weak it may be impossible to restore. $2,000, if American $10,000

◀ DECORATION
Decoration can help with dating. This piece shows a technique known as bright-cutting, which was popular in the late 18th century. $1,500-2,000. If American $15,000

WHAT TO LOOK FOR
● Check the point where the handle joins the body to make sure it's secure.
● Examine the hinge on the lid – make sure it is not weak or restored.
● Make sure the spout isn't split.
● Breathe on the finial and around the spout and hinges – this helps to show repairs.

◀ STYLES
Some 19th century teapots were so elaborate it is hard to imagine they were ever used! This tree stump teapot made in 1814 copies a ceramic form and is covered with undulating foliage and has a handle made to look like bark. $2,000-3,000

COFFEE POTS

THIS 1734 COFFEE POT COULD HAVE BEEN USED EITHER FOR COFFEE OR CHOCOLATE, BUT POTS WHICH HAVE A REMOVABLE FINIAL, WITH A HOLE IN THE LID FOR A SWIZZLE STICK TO STIR THE SEDIMENT, ARE USUALLY TERMED "CHOCOLATE" POTS.

PAUL DE LAMERIE
One of the most acclaimed silversmiths of the 18th century, Paul de Lamerie was a French Huguenot (Protestant refugee) who built up a prosperous London business. Clients included rich Americans and his most famous pieces were very lavishly decorated.

MAKERS
The mark of a well-known maker adds to the value of any piece – this pot was made by Paul de Lamerie, and is worth over $50,000; a pot by a lesser name could cost $2,000-4,000. If American $50,000+ depending on maker and history.

● Other famous English names to look out for are: the Bateman family, the Fox family, Philip Rollos and Paul Storr.

MARKS
These should be in a line by the handle, or in a group or scattered on the base. Lids should also be marked.

▶ ALTERATIONS
During the 19th century, covered tankards (see left) became unfashionable and some were converted into coffee pots. Converted pots (see right) are illegal in England unless the additions are marked. In America Colonial tankards were made into pitchers by adding a spout.

MUGS & JUGS

A huge variety of cups, tankards and jugs have been made over the centuries. They remain highly popular with today's collectors. The vast majority of those you are likely to come across today date from the 18th century or later. Although silver is relatively robust, jugs and mugs have often been well-used, and condition is important to value – so examine pieces carefully before buying them.

Other factors which affect the value of mugs and jugs are common to any type of silver – namely quality, date and maker. You will find that a mug marked by a known maker will invariably cost more than an unmarked one, and elaborate decoration will also raise the price – although be careful because many once-plain 18th century tankards (lidded mugs) were elaborately decorated in the Victorian period and these are less desirable than a plain piece in original condition.

MUGS		TANKARDS	
 **BALUSTER CANN,** *c.*1740 $1,500-2,000. If American $2,000-5,000		 **EARLY 18TH CENTURY TANKARD** $2,000-5,000. If American $10,000- 100,000+ depending on maker and history.	
WHEN AND WHY	Made from the late 17thC, early mugs mirror the shapes of pottery – with bulbous bases and slender necks; those made in the early 18thC had straight tapered sides, later the baluster shape became popular, and pottery copied silver forms.	Most date from *c.*1660-*c.*1780. Made for drinking ale, they became less prevalent as wine and spirits became more popular. Georgian tankards are usually plain, some have armorials. Tankards made in the 19thC (often for presentation) were usually very elaborate.	
WHAT TO LOOK FOR	**Marks:** until the end of the 18thC, in a group under the base; later pieces are marked in a line by the handle. <ul><li>Check handles and rims for signs of weakening or splitting.</li><li>Examine sides for signs of erased armorials (see p89).</li></ul>	**Marks:** on one side of body or base and on lid; earlier tankards have marks in a line on top of the lid; later they are in a group inside. <ul><li>Check handle sockets, they may have become weak.</li><li>Examine thickness of cover – if it's domed, and thin, it may have been reworked from a flat lid.</li></ul>	
OTHER STYLES			

BEWARE
This tankard has been turned into a pitcher and embellished with elaborate foliate chasing during the 19th century. In England such conversions must have later marks on any added parts such as the spout. Generally the decorations on Victorian conversions are not well integrated into the design and the proportions are not as pleasing as authentic originals. $1,000-1,500

JUGS

CREAM JUG, 1730
$800-2,000. If American $2,000+

SAUCEBOATS

GEORGE III SAUCEBOAT, 1761
$3,000-4,000. If American $5,000-10,000+

Made from the 16thC for shaving or for serving liquids such as beer, wine, water, milk or cream. Earlier jugs occasionally had hinged lids, but by the mid-18thC many small open jugs on three legs were made for serving milk or cream.	Earliest date from *c.*1710 and have a spout at each end and two handles on either side of the centre. Later, shallow jug-like sauce boats with central pedestal feet were popular. Three small feet were used in mid-18thC, after which central bases returned to favor.	WHEN AND WHY
Marks: should be on the base or on body, near handle, or under spout. Lidded jugs should have a full set of marks on the body and a maker's mark and lion passant only on the lid – a full set of marks on the lid means it was probably once a tankard! ● Many of these were made out of casters – look for thin silver and hammer marks.	**Marks:** usually underneath in a straight line, those made in the 1770s sometimes have marks under the lip. ● Check legs aren't bent or pushed through the body. ● Examine handles – they can be vulnerable to stress. ● Look at rims – those without applied borders can split.	WHAT TO LOOK FOR

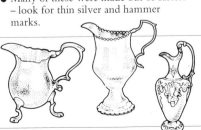

OTHER STYLES

CADDIES & CASTERS

Don't be shocked by the extravagance and cost of the caddies on this page – tea was once so expensive that it was drunk only in the wealthiest homes, and the caddies for storing this precious commodity were intended as objects for display as much as for storage. Caddies were usually kept in the drawing room; some had detachable caps for measuring the tea, while others were even fitted with lock and key to protect their precious contents from dishonest servants!

Caddies are rare in American silver and can be expensive.

Casters played an essential role in fashionable dining rooms when liberal quantities of spices and seasonings were essential to disguise the flavor of stale food. Early casters had straight sides, baluster casters were made from c.1705 becoming taller during the century. Most were originally made in pairs or sets and today these are particularly sought after.

▶ **CADDIES**
Sets of caddies always command a premium. This set of two caddies and a sugar box would be particularly valuable because each piece has its original arms and it comes with its fitted box. $10,000–15,000

▲ **MARKS**
Bodies and lids should be fully hallmarked, although caddies with detachable lids c.1700, as here, are often unmarked. $2,000–3,000. Very rare in America, $30,000+

WHAT TO LOOK FOR
This caddy has three key features you should look for on other pieces:
● high quality decoration
● a maker's mark
● date marks of the 18th century – 19th century caddies are usually less valuable. $2,500–3,500

▲ **CASTERS**
Made to hold sugar, pepper and dry mustard, the shape of casters changed little from c.1705. Better quality ones, such as this, have elaborately pierced covers. This is one of a set of three by well-known maker David Tanqueray in 1713 and is worth over $3,000 Simple pepper pots $400. If American, $2,000+

SALVERS & TRAYS

The difference between salvers and trays is that trays have handles while salvers do not. Both were used as presentation pieces and for practical purposes, and good ones are always popular with collectors. Many salvers survive from *c*.1700 onwards, but trays were not made until the end of the 18th century. Those decorated with elaborate borders will probably cost more than simpler ones.

Salvers and trays often had a coat of arms, crest, or both, engraved in the centre – if the arms belong to a famous family this can increase value two or three times because it provides an insight into the previous ownership and history.

THIS TRAY WAS MADE IN 1806. THE OVAL SHAPE IS TYPICAL OF THE PERIOD. $7,000–10,000

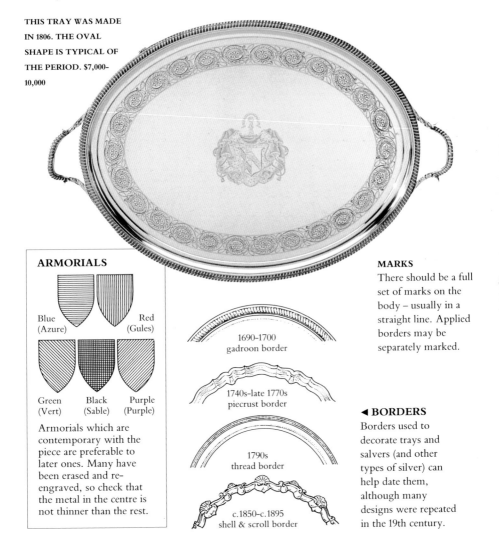

ARMORIALS

Blue (Azure) Red (Gules)

Green (Vert) Black (Sable) Purple (Purple)

Armorials which are contemporary with the piece are preferable to later ones. Many have been erased and re-engraved, so check that the metal in the centre is not thinner than the rest.

1690–1700 gadroon border

1740s–late 1770s piecrust border

1790s thread border

c.1850–c.1895 shell & scroll border

MARKS

There should be a full set of marks on the body – usually in a straight line. Applied borders may be separately marked.

◀ BORDERS

Borders used to decorate trays and salvers (and other types of silver) can help date them, although many designs were repeated in the 19th century.

FLATWARE

Knives, forks and spoons are called "flat-ware". Depending on your budget there are many ways of collecting flatware. Complete services, usually settings for 12, may seem expensive, but spoons and forks in the most common patterns, such as Old English, Fiddle, or Hanoverian are relatively easy to find, and it's often far

less costly to build up a service piecemeal. Flatware services do not usually include knives. These often had thin metal handles which may become worn; most collectors prefer reproductions, which are more hardwearing and robust. With the exception of spoons, 18th century American flatware is rare.

▶ APOSTLE SPOONS

Apostle spoons (so-called because the handle is decorated with the figure of an Apostle), are among the most valuable spoons. Have been faked by reshaping ordinary 18th century spoons – you can spot these by the stiffness of the figure. $500-2,000

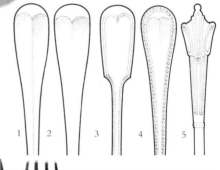

▼ PATTERNS

Different patterns are identifiable by their names; these are some of the most popular ones which have been repeated continually since they were first made. The date of flatware can affect their price even more drama-tically than other types of silver.

1 Hanovarian   2 Old English
3 Fiddle thread   4 Beaded
5 Albany

1   2   3   4   5

▲ OLD ENGLISH PATTERN

The most desirable services contain a dozen tablespoons, table forks, dessert spoons, dessert forks and teaspoons. This 77-piece Old English pattern service has the added bonus of a basting spoon and other serving pieces and this will increase its value. $5,000-8,000

BEWARE

Badly worn forks are virtually impossible to restore and are worth only scrap value. Only the fork on the left is in good condition. The one in the centre is badly worn, the other has been trimmed to disguise the damage.

CANDLESTICKS

Even though we no longer depend on candlelight for illumination, nothing graces a dining table more elegantly than a pair of silver candlesticks. Most candlesticks and candelabra were originally made in pairs or larger sets. Expect to pay more than double for a pair of candlesticks than for two single ones – even if they're the same design and size! To be a true "pair", candlesticks must be made by the same maker at the same date.

THIS TYPICAL MID-18TH CENTURY CANDLESTICK WAS MADE BY CASTING THE SEPARATE SECTIONS – BASE, STEM AND SOCKET – IN MOLDS. CAST CANDLESTICKS ARE	USUALLY MORE DESIRABLE THAN "LOADED" ONES, WHICH WERE MADE FROM THIN SHEETS OF SILVER FILLED WITH PITCH TO GIVE WEIGHT. $2,500-5,000 (A PAIR). AMERICAN $50,000

BASES
Sheet candlesticks are marked in a line above the base, cast ones are marked in the well, or under each corner.

NOZZLE OR BOBECHE
Nozzles should have the maker's mark and lion passant.

SOCKET
If the seam on the stem and socket is not in alignment, the candlestick has been heavily repaired. Here you can see the lion passant mark on the socket.

STEMS
During the 18th century stems became progressively taller; early candlesticks rarely measure more than 13cm/7in; this mid-18th century one is 25cm/10in.

◀ CHAMBER STICKS
These were used to light the way to bed, and unlike other candlesticks, are usually sold singly. This one was made in the 1780s and like many is fitted with a snuffer. $1,000-1,500

▲ CANDELABRA
The separate parts are frequently replaced – four nozzles on this pair are replacements, but the candelabra were made by John Scofield, an eminent 18th century maker, so the price would still be $25,000+

MISCELLANEOUS SILVER

If you want to collect on a modest budget, the vast array of small novel objects made from silver can provide an ideal collecting area. Look carefully in the display cabinets of a general antiques shop, or at a silver auction, and among the pieces you are likely to find are pincushions, card cases, nutmeg graters, vinaigrettes, snuff boxes, sewing cases, glove stretchers, letter openers, match safes and coin cases – to name a few! When you examine the marks you'll find Birmingham's anchor mark appears again and again because from the late 18th century silversmiths in this area produced small silver items by the thousands. Usually, the least expensive pieces tend to be those produced during the 19th century, earlier objects are scarcer and can be high priced.

▶ SNUFF BOXES
The decoration of small boxes has a huge bearing on their price; hunting scenes are particularly sought after – this silver gilt snuff box, made in 1828, would be worth over $1,000–2,000

▶ VINAIGRETTES
Vinaigrettes such as these were used for aromatic salts, vinegar, or perfume and are smaller than snuff boxes, although equally in demand. $1,000+

▶ DECORATION
A piece of silver decorated with a recognizable scene is especially desirable. This Victorian pin tray shows Windsor Castle – one of the most popular views; St Paul's Cathedral or scenes of Edinburgh are also desirable. $700+

WHAT TO LOOK FOR:
Silver boxes
● Check the hinge isn't damaged.
● Make sure the marks on the base are the same as those on the lid – if they don't match, the box may have been altered.

BEWARE
Sometimes snuff boxes are turned into vinaigrettes by adding grilles – and vinaigrettes are turned into pill boxes by removing the grilles! Snuff boxes are turned into compacts by adding mirrors.

▶ MIRRORS

Like most silver-framed mirrors, this 18th century one is part of a dressing table set. Its unusually fine quality is reflected in the price – over $200,000 for the set! During the late 19th/early 20th century less expensive mirrors were made from wooden frames covered with velvet and decorated with die stamped silver. These are often badly worn and difficult to clean but still highly sought after.

DIE STAMPING

Die stamped silver is patterned by pressing solid metal molds together on either side of sheet silver – the technique made it relatively inexpensive to mass-produce elaborate decoration and was much used in the 19th century.

▲ ART NOUVEAU SILVER

Silver items reflecting the Art Nouveau style, marked by well known makers or retailers, are becoming increasingly collectible. This box, with its typical Art Nouveau motif on the lid, was made for Liberty & Co. and would be worth $1,000-1,500

SILVER DECORATION

Small silver is decorated in a wide variety of ways. Some of the most common techniques are:

BRIGHT CUTTING: a type of faceted engraving.

CHASING AND EMBOSSING: patterns made by hammering or punching.

CUT–CARD DECORATION: flat shapes added to the body.

FILIGREE: objects made from silver wire.

▲ SILVER AND GLASS

Glass and silver are often combined to produce some highly decorative objects, but before buying any silver and glass object remember to check that the glass is not broken as it can be costly to replace, especially if shaped. This 1911 Ramsden & Carr silver and enamel case contains its original glass bottle. $2,000+

OTHER METALS

Pewter, brass, copper, wrought iron, Sheffield plate and electroplate are just some of the most common metals that have been used to make a wide variety of decorative and utilitarian objects throughout the centuries. Dating unmarked metal objects can be a potential minefield if you're not sure what to look for. The style of a metal object rarely provides a reliable way of deciding when it was made because many early designs were copied in the 19th and 20th centuries. Look for signs of wear and tear consistent with age: the undersides of objects should be covered with a fine patina of scratches and the edges of plates and hollow wares should be worn smooth. Treat anything with sharp edges or which looks as though it's in perfect condition with suspicion. American metalwork often follows English precedent, and sometimes incorporates continental traditions creating a unique American style.

◀ **PEWTER**
Pewter, or "poor man's silver" as it's sometimes known, is an alloy mainly made of tin with varying proportions of copper, lead and antimony. Pieces in poor condition are less desirable; this c.1780 flagon has an attractive acorn finial and domed cover typical of the period, and is worth $700–1,000. If American 18thC rare; worth $15,000–20,000

HOW OLD IS IT?

- Pewter left uncleaned for years develops a characteristic dull glowing patina.
- Early English and American pewter is usually marked with the maker's stamp.
- Tavern pewter made after c.1826 should be marked with capacity.

▲ **BRASS**
Old brass objects, such as this George III candlestick, often reflect the styles of silver objects of the same date. Pieces marked with makers' stamps are especially desirable; this candlestick is marked by E. Berry, and is worth $1,000–1,500; pairs $3,000+.

Old Sheffield plate was made from a thin layer of silver fused onto a sheet of copper. This type of plate was used from c.1760 as a less expensive alternative to silver. Although highly collectible, Sheffield plate remains good value; this c.1810 novelty tea urn is worth $1,000–1,500.

● You can usually identify old Sheffield plate by its slightly pinkish tinge caused by areas of silver wearing thin, revealing the copper beneath.

▶ COPPER

If you find a piece of metalware marked with the twisted rope symbol of 19th-century manufacturers Perry, Son & Co., you may be in luck and have an unusual piece by Dr Christopher Dresser, one of the most influential designers of the Victorian period. This jug, a striking Dresser design is worth $2,000-3,000+; if electroplate $200-300.

▲ ELECTROPLATE

● The technique of applying a layer of silver over a nickel or alloy base was developed in the mid-19th century.

● Electroplate is susceptible to wear – you can see where the silver has worn thin on this corkscrew. $200-300

● You can have pieces replated but this gives an unnaturally bright appearance which is far less desirable.

Glass is a fascinating and accessible collecting area. Despite the fragility of the substance, glass from the 18th century and later is relatively easy to find, and plain objects can still be inexpensive.

The precise origins of glass are unknown; it was made in ancient Egypt, Syria and Rome. The basic material was made from heating and fusing silica (usually sand) with a flux (potash or soda) and a stabilizer (usually lime).

Drinking glasses, made in large numbers throughout the 18th century, have long been popular with collectors. The value of European glass depends on the rarity of its decorations (very little 18th century American glass is decorated). Many of the more valuable types of 18th century glass have been faked so always buy from a reputable source, or take expert advice when in doubt.

Colorful glass of the 19th century is also increasingly popular. Many new glass-making techniques were introduced during the 19th century and colors became more varied. Cameo and overlay glass are two of the most attractive types to look for, although the best marked examples can be expensive. Unmarked 19th century glass is still reasonably priced, and 19th century table glass can be less expensive than modern equivalents.

BASICS

There are three main types of glass:

SODA GLASS
Made in Venice from the 13th century. The soda was derived from burnt seaweed, and gave the molten glass a malleable quality which allowed glassmakers to create very elaborate shapes.

POTASH GLASS
Potash glass was made in Northern Europe. The potash was derived from burnt wood and bracken. Potash glass was particularly suited to cutting and engraving.

LEAD GLASS
Made from potash with the addition of lead oxide (instead of lime), this glass, developed by George Ravenscroft, was used in England and Ireland from the late 17th century, and in Europe from the late 18th century. Lead glass is heavy and clear and therefore is well suited to cutting.

DECORATION
Decoration on glass can add substantially to its value.

The main decorative techniques used are:
- Cutting
- Enamelling
- Gilding
- Engraving

CUTTING
Cut facets in glass emphasize its refractive (light transmitting) qualities. Cut decoration can help with dating. The earliest patterns were shallow surface cuts. Patterns became increasingly elaborate in the late 18th and early 19th centuries (see p100-101).

ENAMELLING
Painting in colored enamels was popular on Venetian glass from the late 15th century and became fashionable in England in the mid-18th century.

An 18th century enamelled wine-glass attributed to William Beilby $6,000-9,000

The best-known English enamellers were the Beilby family. There are two types of enamelling.

● **Fire enamelling:** the enamel was painted on the surface of the glass, and the glass fired to fix the decoration. This is the most permanent and usual form of enamelling.

● **Cold enamelling:** also known as cold painting, involved painting the glass without firing. This technique has the disadvantage that the enamelling wears off easily, and was mainly used on inexpensive items.

GILDING

Gold decoration can be applied to the surface of glass in a number of different ways. The most permanent method of gilding is by firing the gold onto the surface of the glass. An alternative method was oil gilding, which involved applying a gold powder or leaf onto an oil base and burnishing. Gilding applied using this method is easily rubbed off.

ENGRAVING

There are four types of engraving:

Diamond point engraving: the design was scratched onto the surface of the glass using a tool with a diamond nib. This technique was used in the 16th century in Venice, and in England in the late 16th-19th century.

A diamond-etched wine glass, Dutch 17th century, $2,000-5,000

Wheel engraving: the design was engraved using small copper wheels of varying diameter which rotated against the surface of the glass. The technique was used in Germany in the 17th century, and became the most common form of engraving in England and America from the 18th century.

Stipple engraving: a fine diamond needle was tapped and drawn on the surface to form a design built up from dots and small lines. This technique was popular in the Netherlands in the 18th century and is also found on English glasses.

A stipple engraved glass, Dutch c.1745 $3,500-5,000

Acid etching: this technique involved covering the surface with varnish, grease or wax, and scratching the design with a needle or sharp tool. The surface was then exposed to hydrofluoric acid which etched the design on the glass. This method was popular in the 19th, early 20th century.

AUTHENTICITY

Fakes of many of the more expensive types of antique glass abound. Victorian glassmakers made imitations of 18th century glass and many fakes have also been produced in the 20th century. These are often discernible in four key ways:

● **Shape and color:** the shape of machine made glass is regular and the glass does not have impurities that give old glass a distinctive tint.

● **Manufacturing method:** hand-blown glass often has a pontil mark – a rough bump under the stem – where it was cut from the pontil rod. Look for vertical tool marks in the bowl left by the jack blades which held the glass while the foot was attached. It may have striations in the glass and the rim may be of uneven thickness.

● **Proportions:** have varied throughout the centuries. On old glasses the foot is usually as wide as the bowl. Wrong proportions may indicate a fake.

DRINKING GLASSES & DECANTERS

Compared with ceramics of the same date, much antique glass remains relatively inexpensive. You can still find sets of six 19th century glasses for under $300 at antiques shops and general auctions, and incredibly, an antique decanter will often cost less than a modern one.

During the 18th century, large numbers of drinking glasses were made. The variety available means that there are many ways of collecting glass. You may decide to focus your collection on, say, air twists, Jacobite glass, cordials, or gilded glass, or you may prefer to simply collect single examples of each type. Simpler 18th century glasses may cost $50–100, but those with elaborate or unusual decoration can be very much more valuable.

SIGNS OF AGE
- a foot that is wider than the rim
- flaws showing the glass was hand-made
- early glass has a bell like ring when tapped
- a bumpy "pontil mark" under the foot
- a greenish or greyish tinge in the glass
- signs of wear on the foot – fine and irregular scratches.

JACOBITE GLASSES
Glasses engraved with roses, doves and oak leaves were made in the 18th century to show secret allegiance to the Old Pretender (James Edward Stuart) and the Young Pretender (Charles Edward Stuart). They are particularly collectible but can be expensive – an especially rare one was sold in 1992 for $100,000. Watch out for fakes.

◀ COLOR TWISTS
Stems with threads of colored glass are keenly sought after; value depends on the number of colors. This one has blue and opaque white twists, and would be worth about $2,000+

▶ GILDED GLASS
Glasses with original, soft 18th century gilding, such as this one, are very desirable, but are rarely seen in perfect condition. $750+

BEWARE
You can spot less desirable later gilding, by its brassier, brighter appearance.

COLLECTORS CATEGORIZE AND VALUE GLASSES ACCORDING TO THE SHAPE AND DECORATION OF THE BOWL, STEM AND FOOT. THIS ONE IS OF MEDIUM QUALITY – IT HAS A PLAIN BOWL AND A RELATIVELY SIMPLE STEM, BUT BECAUSE IT IS LARGER THAN MOST (MEASURING 9IN) IT IS WORTH ABOUT $400-1,200.

This is a multi-knopped stem, so called because of the series of knops which make up its stem; some stems have only one knop, which may contain a tear drop of air, other stems are decorated with air twists.

1   2   3
1 Multiple spiral
2 Single series
3 Double series

1   2
1 Conical foot
2 Domed foot

The bowl of this 1720 glass is a round funnel shape; other bowl shapes are shown below.

1 Bucket   2 Waisted
3 Conical   4 Bell
5 Ogee   6 Trumpet

This glass has a domed foot, characteristic of many early glasses; others have conical feet. Folded or turned under feet were common until 1810. Check for underparts ground down because of damage.

DECANTERS
Some decanters have engraved or gilded labels describing their contents. This one is made of "Bristol" blue glass – Bristol is associated with colo-red decanters, but not all were made there. $250-800. Beware of Spanish fakes.

CUT & PRESSED GLASS

Nothing makes glass sparkle more brightly in candlelight than cut decoration, and this is one reason why cutting has long been one of the most popular ways of embellishing all types of glass objects. Early glass was simply cut by hand, in fairly shallow patterns, but gradually patterns became deeper and designs more elaborate, and by c.1830 mechanized wheel cutting became the norm. As demand increased for inexpensive glass wares, press-molded glass, which looked like cut glass but cost far less, became popular. Although 18th century cut glass is increasing in popularity and price; it can still be good value. If you want to collect cut glass to use on the dining table look out for jellies, custards, sweetmeat dishes, fruit bowls and candlesticks; many of these are still relatively inexpensive, especially if you buy them singly.

▶ **IRISH GLASS**
If you see a piece of glass which looks lopsided the chances are it's Irish! Glass made in Ireland, such as this compote, can also often be identified by its greyish tinge and the typical shallow diamond cutting. $1,000 if 12in in diameter.

CUT OR PRESSED?
Cut glass is usually far more desirable and valuable than pressed glass, and there are several ways of identifying it:
● sharply faceted decoration
● no mold lines inside.

CUT GLASS PATTERNS
These are some of the most common cut glass patterns used during the 18th and 19th centuries. However, because they have been repeated in the 20th century, the pattern alone is not a reliable guarantee of authenticity – you should also look at the color of the glass and for irregularities that show it's hand made.

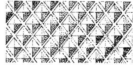
Plain sharp diamonds

Strawberry diamonds

Pillar flutes

Cross-cut diamonds

Star cutting

Fine diamonds

THE HANDKERCHIEF TEST

Plain early glass has sometimes been decorated with later engraving to make it seem more valuable. To check the decoration is authentic, drop a white handkerchief in the glass – old engraving will look dark and grey, new engraving white and powdery.

● A handkerchief is also useful to reveal the color of the glass.

▲ PRESSED GLASS
During the Victorian period clear and colored pressed glass plates were often made to commem-orate important events; this one celebrates Queen Victoria's Golden Jubilee. $75-100

▼ LATER CUT GLASS
Extensive sets of less elaborate turn of the century cut glass can still be very affordable. This is part of a set of 89 items made *c.*1900; the whole set would cost $1,500-2,000.

◀ CRYSTAL
Engraved lead glass, cut and polished to simulate the natural facets of rock crystal is known as crystal and became popular during the late 19th and early 20th century. $200

COLORED GLASS

Colored drinking glasses and decanters were produced in relatively small quantities in England during the 18th century, but 18th century styles were much copied in the late 19th/early 20th century and some later versions are so convincing that even experienced collectors can be confused (see p98 for signs of authenticity). Most of the colored glass you are likely to come across dates from after c.1800, when many lavishly decorated glass objects were made both in this country and on the Continent.

WHAT TO LOOK FOR
- Pieces marked by the workshops of Thomas Webb, W.H.B. & J. Richardson and Stevens & Williams.
- Larger pieces.
- Multiple layers of glass.
- High quality design – Neo-classical figures are especially desirable.

◀ OPALINE GLASS
Although at first glance this goblet looks as though it's made from porcelain, it's an example of English opaline glass made c.1850. Much opaline glass was also made in France; quality can vary – the best pieces are made from lead crystal and are very heavy. $500+

▶ CAMEO GLASS
Cameo glass – made by overlaying the base color with a layer of contrasting glass which was then carved to reveal the color underneath – is one of the more expensive types of 19th century colored glass. This large bottle has a silver top, and is worth $1,500-2,000. Even miniature bottles can be worth $400+ to $4,000+.

▲ RUBY GLASS
Ruby glass, sometimes made from tinted glass or from clear glass with a ruby stain on the surface, was produced both in Bohemia, England and America. The value of the elaborate piece (left) with the silver gilt handles is $2,500-3,000; the simpler jug (right) is worth $500-800. An American ruby glass goblet with an American view, $2,500

PAPERWEIGHTS

The most sought-after antique paper-weights are those made by famous French factories Baccarat, Clichy and St Louis during the middle years of the 19th century. Patterns were built up from tiny slices of differently colored rods or canes of glass, set in a mold and covered in clear glass. The size can vary from under 2in to 4in or more.

BACCARAT
YOU CAN OFTEN IDENTIFY THE MAKER OF A PAPERWEIGHT BY THE TYPE OF RODS IT CONTAINS AND THE WAY THEY ARE ARRANGED. THIS ONE INCLUDES SILHOUETTES OF A DOG, A HORSE AND A DEER, WHICH ARE TYPICAL OF THE BACCARAT FACTORY. $5,000-7,000

IDENTIFYiNG MARKS

Contemporary paperweights are generally signed and dated. Antique paperweights are rarely signed and dated. The exception is Baccarat which sometimes includes signed and datedcanes – this one is marked *B 1848*. St Louis and Clichy paperweights are also sometimes marked with initials.

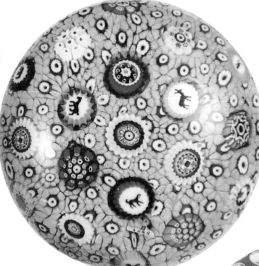

MILLEFIORI
Millefiori ("thous-and flower") paperweights are so-called because their canes resemble a carpet of flowers.

▲ **ST LOUIS**
Large single flower heads were much used by the St Louis factory. Sometimes flowers were laid on a criss-cross lattice, known as *latticinio*. $5,000+ if perfect.

▲ **CLICHY**
Clichy weights can often be identified by the characteristic rose they contain. This rare one is worth $4,000–6,000; more common types fetch $1,000+.

▲ **OVERLAY WEIGHTS**
Some rare weights, such as this one made by Baccarat, contain a layer of opaque glass through which windows are cut to reveal the design beneath. This one would be worth $3,000 or more.

Clocks have been appreciated and treasured from at least the 17th century to the present day. Unlike many other types of antiques, clocks are unique in that they are "working" antiques. You can appreciate them both for their visual appeal and for their technical mastery and they also serve a useful purpose telling time.

If you're a novice collector thinking of investing in a clock, it's probably best to buy one in working order. Most clocks can be repaired, but restoring a "bargain" can be a laborious and expensive business, and unless the problem is very straightforward it's often cheaper in the long run to buy a clock which has been properly overhauled by a skilled clockmaker.

Most clocks are relatively easy to date and identify because they were signed by their maker on the dial and movement, and records of most makers have survived. A clock's visual appeal, however, lies largely in its case, which usually reflects contemporary furniture styles.

Despite their popularity, clocks are available at a wide range of prices. Value depends on the maker, movement, case and condition. Plain carriage clocks and simple table clocks are available from about $300, and a late 19th century English long case clock around $1,200; American long case clocks $2,500+.

BASICS

There are three key elements which you should assess before buying a clock:
- the mechanism, or movement
- the dial
- the case.

MOVEMENTS

The movement consists of a system of brass and steel wheels and gears, known as the train. It is usually housed between two brass plates.

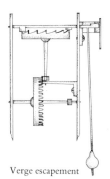

Verge escapement

The escapement: is the part of the movement which controls the speed at which a clock runs.

Verge or balance wheel escapement: the balance wheel was used on lantern clocks until c.1670. The oscillating balance wheel releases the two pallets or "flags" on the vertical bar, which engage the toothed wheel. The verge escapement is similar but has a short pendulum.

Anchor escapement: was first used in longcases from c.1670, and became standard for long case and bracket clocks.

Balance wheel

The anchor engages with the teeth of the escape wheel. Clocks with an anchor may have a long or short pendulum.

PENDULUM

Weight-driven and spring-driven clocks usually have a pendulum to control the clock's speed. The pendulum is a brass or steel rod with a metal disc, or bob, at the bottom. Adjusting the position of the bob on the rod alters the timekeeping of the clock.

DIALS

A chapter ring
B subsidiary dial
C calendar aperture
D applied corner spandrels
E winding holes
F hour hand
G minute hand
H dial arch
I engraved boss
J "matted" center

The dial is the face of the clock and is attached to the movement by a number of brass "feet". A dial has an important bearing on price. Clocks with replaced dials are much less desirable. There are four main types of dial:

Brass dials: this is the earliest type of dial, used on lantern, bracket and longcases. These have the hours engraved onto a detachable chapter ring.

Painted metal dials: found on most clocks after c.1800. These became more elaborate in the 19th century.

Painted wooden dials: found on English dial clocks, tavern clocks and Continental and American clocks. If authentic, the wood should show some signs of cracking caused by changes in temperature.

Enamelled metal dials: common on carriage clocks and other types of French clocks. They are made from enamel fired on thin copper sheet.

HANDS

Early clocks only have one hand (for hours), but from c.1660 most have a minute and an hour hand. Second hands are usually shown on a subsidiary dial. Hands are usually made from blued steel, although gilded brass is found from c.1790. Until c.1740 the hour hand was elaborate; the minute hand was longer and simpler.

● Replacement hands are acceptable if they are in the right style.

CASES

The case houses the dial and movement. Knowledge of materials and styles is useful in dating a clock and in assessing its value.

Wooden cases: these were introduced in the 17th century. Many cases are covered with thin veneers of wood. The most common woods are ebony, walnut, mahogany and rosewood. Wooden cases may be decorated with marquetry (patterns made from different woods see p44),

lacquer, applied metal mounts, brass inlay (on rosewood cases), or a combination of tortoiseshell and brass (boulle work).

Metal cases: Brass is the most common metal; all carriage clocks are brass-cased. Old brass is uneven and shows marks left by the casting process; modern rolled brass is of uniform thickness. Brass cases may be elaborately engraved or decorated with enamel colors.

SIGNATURES

Most clocks are signed, although a signature is not always a guarantee that the clock was made by the maker whose signature it bears. 19th century clocks may be signed by the retailer rather than the maker. Genuine signatures are usually found in the following places:

● until 1690: along the bottom of the dial plate.
● from 1690–1720: on the chapter ring.
● after 1720: on the chapter ring; or on the boss in the arch or on an applied plaque.

BRACKET CLOCKS

Not all "bracket" clocks stood on wall brackets. Clocks of this type were also used for tables and mantelpieces. Nowadays the term is used to describe all clocks with short pendulums and spring-driven mechanisms. These clocks are also sometimes called "spring", "mantel" or "table" clocks.

Bracket clocks were made from c.1660, the earliest with square brass dials; by the beginning of the 18th century, arched dials became more common. Among the most

often seen English bracket clocks are those with mahogany veneered cases. Large numbers were produced from the late 18th and early 19th century, mainly in London, and you can still find clocks of this type for around $3,000-6,000. Also frequently seen are French 19th century clocks, which were made in a wide variety of shapes. Many of these incorporate such lavish decoration that you may need to take a second look before you realize they are clocks not sculpture.

▼ **EARLY BRACKETS**
Early (pre-1700) bracket clocks, such as this c.1695 one, are usually the most valuable. You can generally identify them by their ebony or walnut cases and decorative square dials. Condition often determines price.

▶ **REGENCY CLOCKS**
Bracket clocks made in the Regency period, usually have signed convex dials, simple brass or blued steel hands, and a mahogany or rosewood case. $3,000.

▲ **FRENCH MANTEL CLOCKS**
Depending on the degree of elaboration, prices for French clocks start at around $1,000. This one is decorated with a bronze figure of a negress (representing Africa) and a gilt panther and tortoise and is worth $8,000+.

MAKERS
The value of a clock is greatly increased if it's signed by a famous maker. The dial and backplate of this clock (above and right) are signed by Thomas Tompion, one of the most famous English clockmakers known as the "father of English clock-making," and it would therefore be worth over $100,000!

MOVEMENTS

Most mahogany brackets originally had a verge escapement (see p104–105): many of these were converted to an anchor escapement but this should not put you off buying if the price is right.

STRIKE/SILENT LEVER

The strike/silent lever controls the striking mechanism and can be turned off without affecting the time keeping.

MAHOGANY BRACKETS

MOST MAHOGANY CLOCKS ARE LARGER THAN EARLIER EBONY OR WALNUT ONES. THIS ONE, WHICH WAS MADE c.1785, IS OF STANDARD SIZE AND MEASURES 51CM/20IN. $7,500

CLOCK CARE

- Carefully dust and wax wooden cases.
- Never attempt to clean brass or silvered dials.
- Ask an expert to oil and clean the clock's mechanism.
- Hold clocks upright if you're moving them from one room to another.
- Secure or remove the pendulum before a long journey.

BEWARE

Check finials; all should match. Many clocks have replaced finials, a minor flaw.

CASES

Both elaborate and simple cases were made from mahogany. This one is fairly simple, but the illustrations below show some of the more elaborate varieties found.

| Lacquer c.1770 ht 25in | Mahogany c.1780 ht 19½in | Mahogany c.1780 ht 20½in | Mahogany c.1795 ht 15¾in | Ebonized c.1810 ht 19in | Mahogany c.1825 ht 26in |

LONG CASE CLOCKS

Perhaps because of their homely appearance and reassuring "tick-tock", long cases, popularly known as "grandfather" clocks, are among the most appealing of all antique clocks. Most long case clocks were made in England from the late 17th-19th centuries, although lesser numbers were also produced in Europe and America. The standard long case runs for 8 days and has an anchor escapement. Like most types of clock, value depends on the quality of the case, movement, dial and maker. If a clock has an unusual or attractively painted dial, or an elaborate marquetry or lacquered case, it will cost more than a run-of-the-mill version. Size can also have a bearing on price. Smaller long cases are usually more expensive than larger ones – and for good reason – taller ones were built to fit in rooms with higher ceilings than in many homes today – so before you buy a long case remember to check it will fit!

DIALS

Originally square, dials became arched in c.1720. Generally 18th century American clocks have brass dials; 19th century painted dials. Brass dials are usually 12in in diameter and have an applied chapter ring (the band showing the numbers) and applied spandrels (corners).

QUICK DIAL CHECK

| square (17thC) | arched (c.1700-19thC) | circular (c.1830) |

▲ **WALNUT LONG CASES**
Some of the earliest long case clocks were covered with walnut veneers over an oak carcass. Cross-banded veneers (a strip laid at right angles to the main veneer) add to value. $20,000

▲ **MARQUETRY**
Floral marquetry was a popular way of decorating long cases between 1680 and 1710. Earlier examples have small inset panels of marquetry decoration; on later ones, such as this, the design covers the entire surface. $15,000

Finials are easily damaged and replacements, though acceptable, are less desirable.

The small dials measure the seconds and the calendar months.

The hands on most long cases are made from "blued" steel – the metal was heated to create the dark color.

The trunk – center section of the case – has a door which opens to allow you to adjust the pendulum and fit the weights. Long cases were designed to stand against a wall, so the backs are made from unfinished wood.

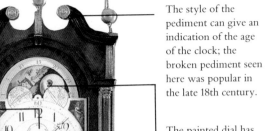

The style of the pediment can give an indication of the age of the clock; the broken pediment seen here was popular in the late 18th century.

The painted dial has attractive figures in the spandrels and a moon disc, showing the phases of the moon, in the arch. Look for crazing (a fine network of cracks) on painted dials as a sign of authenticity. Repainted dials are less desirable in the USA.

NAMES TO LOOK OUT FOR

This clock is signed by a Birmingham clock-maker named Edward White. London-made long cases are particularly sought after. In America clocks signed by David Rittenhouse, the Willard family and apprentices bring a premium.

MAHOGANY LONG CASES

MAHOGANY WAS USED TO MAKE LONG CASES FROM THE MID 18TH CENTURY UNTIL THE 19TH CENTURY. BECAUSE THIS ONE (C.1785) IS FAIRLY ELABORATE IT'S WORTH AROUND $5,000, BUT YOU CAN FIND SIMPLE 19TH CENTURY VERSIONS FROM ABOUT $2,000+.

The wood on the base and plinth should match the rest of the case. Long case clocks cut off at the top and bottom have reduced value.

CARRIAGE CLOCKS

Few people today would think of packing a carriage clock when they go on a journey, even though, as one of the earliest types of travelling clock, this is what they were made for. Carriage clocks usually have brass cases and were fitted with handles so they could be more easily carried – hence their name – many also came with a leather travelling case. Nearly all carriage clocks were made in France during the 19th and early years of the 20th century; a few were also produced in England. Carriage clocks are among the least expensive types of antique clocks available. You can still buy less elaborate models for around $500-800 although quality ones may cost over $3,000.

CHECKLIST OF TYPICAL FRENCH CARRIAGE CLOCK FEATURES

- white enamel dial
- black numerals
- stamped mark or signature on the backplate
- 8-day spring driven movement
- bevelled glass panels
- blued steel hands.

QUALITY FEATURES

- engraved case
- panelled *cloisonné* or porcelain case
- subsidiary dials.

FIRMS & MAKERS TO LOOK OUT FOR

Auguste (active from 1840) French
Abraham-Louis Breguet (1747-1823) French
Achille and Louis Brocot (active 19thC) French
Dejardin (active 19thC) French
Pierre and Alfred Drocourt (1860-89) French
Frodsham family (19/20thC) English
Paul Garnier (*b.*1801-*d.*1869) French
Japy (1772-early 20thC) French
F.A. Margaine (*c.*1870-1912) French
E. Maurice (active 1880s) French
James McCabe (19thC) English
Soldano (*c.*1855-80) French

◀ REPEAT BUTTONS

Some carriage clocks have a repeat button on the top of the case: when the button is pressed the clock repeats the last hour struck. This one was made by Henri Jacot *c.*1890. $800-2,000

◀ ENGRAVED CASES

Engraved-case carriage clocks are more valuable than plain ones. Look for elaborate decoration which covers as much of the case as possible. This one was made by Le Roy & Fils *c.*1865. $1,000-5,000

◀ SUBSIDIARY DIALS

Clocks with subsidiary dials are especially desirable. This English carriage clock has an alarm dial; some also have dials showing seconds or the days of the week. $1,000+

NOVELTY & SKELETON CLOCKS

Novelty clocks, which tell the time in a particularly unusual or intriguing way, are among the most fascinating of all clocks. Most of those seen today date from the 19th century when they were produced by French, Swiss and English makers. The value of a novelty clock is dependent on rarity, appearance and the complexity of moving features, rather than the clock mechanism. Condition is of particular importance, as broken novelty clocks can be extremely expensive to repair.

▶ **MYSTERY CLOCKS**
This is one of the most common types of novelty clock. The movement, concealed in the base, rotates the figure slightly from left to right, and this motion makes the pendulum swing, even though the figure holding it seems unconnected to the mechanism. $3,000+

◀ **AUTOMATON CLOCKS**
Automaton clocks are among the most varied and valuable of novelty clocks. This one is relatively simple – it contains a bird which every hour sings a melodic nightingale song, while flapping its wings, turning its head, and opening its beak. $6,000–10,000

▶ **SKELETON CLOCKS**
English-made skeleton clocks, in which as much of the working mechanism as possible is visible, are usually far more complex and elaborate than those made in France. This typically elaborate one (with protective glass dome removed) dates from c.1870. It was made by J. Smith & Sons and is worth $10,000–15,000.

The only difference between a rug and a carpet is size. Rugs are usually small enough to hang on the wall. Any larger than 5 by 8 feet is usually referred to as a carpet. Broadly speaking, rugs and carpets fall into two main groups; serious collectors' rugs, and decorative rugs. Older rugs are mainly of interest to collectors because they are more diverse in pattern and richer in color than more recently made rugs. More recently-made rugs and carpets are chiefly of interest to decorators.

All rugs are categorized by their place of origin or the tribe that made them. To be able to identify the difference between, say, a Kazak and a Kuba, you need to familiarize yourself with the various distinctive colors, patterns, motifs and weaves characteristic of each type.

The size, richness of the colors, fineness of the knots, intricacy of design and condition are all important when valuing rugs. Collectible rugs should be hand-made. To check, look on the reverse – you should be able to see the design on the back as well as on the front. Next, part the pile and look at the knots, if there are loops rather than knots this indicates a machine-made rug of very little interest to collectors. Most old rugs cost much more than modern replicas. Woven kelims can be found for as little as $700+.

BASICS

MATERIALS

The foundation material of a rug (the warp and weft) is usually wool, cotton, or (rarely) silk. The best quality wool is fine, soft and shiny. Inferior quality wool is coarse and lacks luster.

COLORS

Color is one of the most important factors in assessing old rugs. The best colors are those made from natural vegetable and insect dyes.

Natural dyes
Blues and reds in most old rugs appear as various shadings. Warm red colors are usually derived from the plant, madder. Blue comes from indigo.

● Sometimes crimson comes from insect dyes such as cochineal. This indicates a date after c.1850 when cochineal was first imported to the East.

Chemical (aniline) dyes These were introduced in 1863: they tend to be sharper in tone, and not as colorfast.

Chromatic dyes These were first used in the early 20th century and come in a wide color range. They can be difficult to distinguish from natural dyes which are generally colorfast, while chromatic dyes fade.

KNOTS

The type of knot used to attach the pile to the warp and weft can help identify where the rug was made. The quality of a rug is reflected by the fineness of the knots which are measured according to their number per square inch. A coarse rug may have 50 to 90 knots per square inch, or 150 to 175 knots per square inch, depending on where it was made; a fine one may have many hundreds. There are two main types of knot:

● Turkish, or Ghiordes; a symmetric knot used in Turkey and tribal groups in Persia and Central Asia.

● Persian or Senneh; an asymmetric knot used in Iran and by some Central Asian groups.

PERSIAN RUGS

Richly colored and exotic, Persian rugs have long been highly sought after; the finest are made from silk and are among the most expensive of all Oriental carpets. Most Persian carpets seen today date from the 19th and 20th centuries and are either tribal village pieces woven both to trade and to use or town-made factory pieces, produced specifically for the Western market.

CARPET CARE

Carpets can be washed with plain warm or cold water and a mild detergent. Snow is a good way of removing dust – cover the rug with snow and brush it off and it will take the dust with it!

◀ PRAYER RUGS
Garden motifs recur in many Persian rugs and are inspired by the Islamic notion of the Garden of Paradise. Prayer rugs – small carpets used to kneel on during prayer – such as this late-19th century one, show the garden through a *mihrab* or arch. $850–10,000+

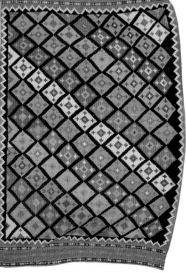

▶ KELIMS
Unlike other types of carpets, kelims are flat-woven and have no knots and no pile. The many modern reproduction kelims are identifiable by bright colors and coarse weave. Old or antique rugs such as this Qashqa'i kelim, which dates from the late 19th century, are finely woven and softly colored. $2,000–3,000+

▲ CONDITION
This Heriz carpet from northwest Persia has areas of repiling, and the outermost borders at each end have been cut and bound; even so, because it is attractively colored with vegetal dyes and a large size – 12ft 2in × 9ft 7in – it is worth $5,000–9,000 if 20th century. If late 19th century $20,000–30,000

CAUCASIAN & TURKISH RUGS

Distinctive geometric designs are a characteristic of many Oriental rugs made in the region between the Black and Caspian Seas. In this rugged mountainous area, known as the Caucasus, carpets were made by villagers using small looms. Each region has its own distinctive designs. Among the most famous and frequently seen Caucasian rugs are Kazaks, Shirvans and Sumaks.

Turkish carpets fall into two distinct groups: those made by nomadic tribal weavers and those made in urban or Imperial factories. Rugs cover a wide spectrum of prices, from expensive silk rugs to cheaper Anatolian kelims, which are still available for a modest outlay.

▼ SOUMACS Soumacs are a type of flat weave and are one of the easiest of the Caucasian rugs to identify because they are flat-woven rather than knotted, but, unlike other kelims, are patterned on one side only.

This is the bottom half of a Soumac bagface – trappings such as bags, saddle covers and tent hangings are always popular with collectors and can be expensive. $800–900; complete $2,000–5,000

▲ KAZAKS Large, bold geometric designs and long fine quality wool are features of Kazak

rugs. These carpets are usually relatively small – this one is 5ft × 3ft 9in – and is worth $3,000–6,000.

KAZAK MOTIFS

Pinwheel   Karachov   Fachralo   Bordjalou

Kazaks are often named according to their distinctive designs. These are some of the most commonly seen motifs.

WHAT TO LOOK FOR

- bright vibrant colors – preferably colored with vegetable dyes (see p112)
- avoid synthetic orange, purple faded to grey, reds that bleed
- good condition, unless very early
- complete rugs – cut down ones are a lot less desirable

IS IT OLD?

- Check the pile with a magnifying glass. If the fading is soft and gradual it's old; if you can see three distinct bands of color the rug may have been artificially aged.
- Lick a handkerchief and rub it on the carpet – dyes which come off copiously may be chemical – an indication that the carpet is not very old.

COLOR FOLKLORE	
RED	happiness
BLACK	rebellion and devastation
BROWN	plentitude, fruitfulness
WHITE	cleanliness, serenity
GREEN	rejuvenation
GOLD	prosperity
WHITE	purity.

▶ LADIKS

The central Anatolian village of Ladik is renowned for its fine-quality prayer rugs (see p113). This one contains a poetic inscription at the base of the niche. $7,500–10,000+

◀ SHIRVANS

Shirvans typically have short pile and small geometric patterns, in which dark blues and strong reds predominate. $4,000–6,000

MODERN RUGS

Modern rugs such as this Azeri, from southeastern Turkey was woven with hand spun yarn colored with natural dyes. This design is adapted from a Heriz area (northwestern Iran) proto-type. These good quality rugs are of interest to decorators. Room size 9ft 5in × 12ft 4in, $6,000. Smaller Azeris $1,000–2,000.

INDIAN & CHINESE RUGS

A prison may seem an unlikely setting for valuable carpet making, but during the 19th century large numbers of woven and pile carpets were made in Indian jails such as Agra, Amritsar and Hyderabad and today the best of them are sought after. Indian carpets often reflect the influence of Persian rugs which were used as a source for some designs. India is also famous for woven *dhurries* – the Indian equivalent of kelims.

The real and imaginary beasts and symbols of power, wealth and good luck which pepper the surface of many Chinese rugs make them highly distinctive – and easy to recognize. Most of those you are likely to come across date from the 19th century or later and were specially made for the Western market.

VALUE POINTS

- Pile Agras are among the most popular with decorators – prices range from $15,000–40,000.
- Indian carpets, with white or yellow grounds are more decorative and desirable than red or blue, which are more common.
- *Dhurries* are the least expensive Indian carpets. Prices range from $3,000–20,000 for large ones.
- Chinese carpets made in the 19th and early 20th centuries usually fall in the $5,000–30,000+ range.
- Chinese carpets with Art Deco designs are less expensive; $4,000–10,000 room size.

▲ INDIAN CARPETS
Carpets made in India for the European market were often extremely large. This Agra measures 19ft 8in × 13ft 11in and is worth $30,000.

▼ CHINESE CARPETS
Traditional motifs seen in Chinese art inspired the patterns seen on rugs made in China: this Ninghsia rug was probably based on Chinese silks. $7,500–15,000 depending on size and condition.

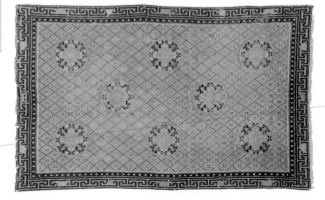

EUROPEAN RUGS

If you visit a sale of Oriental rugs or a specialist carpet dealer you may be surprised at the large number of European-made carpets for sale. Needlework rugs are among the most popular and abundant Western rugs. Many were made by ladies of the leisure class from the 16th century onwards, but some were commercially produced during the 19th century. Designs are colorful and extremely varied; some patterns were adapted from Oriental rugs, others were derived from printed textiles.

Flower-filled rugs made in Aubusson in France and the surrounding villages have also enjoyed a huge upsurge in popularity. If the price of an Aubusson is out of your reach, slightly worn small rugs or fragments of larger ones are more affordable.

AUBUSSON RUGS
AUBUSSONS SUCH AS THIS (MADE c.1890) WERE WOVEN ON A LOOM AND HAVE NO PILE. $20,000-50,000

PATTERN
The design was built up one color at a time, each color woven back and forth only in the area required. When a new color was added a vertical split was left between the wefts, which was stitched up by hand afterwards.

BORDERS
This border has been cut or folded back; Aubussons were originally made for the ceiling not the floor and followed the lines of the architecture of the room.

NEEDLEWORK RUGS
The pleasant floral design, good condition, and unfaded colors are all signs of good quality which add to the desirability of this mid-19th century needlework rug. If 6 × 9ft, $8,000-12,000.

Arts and crafts, Art Nouveau and Art Deco were the results of the most significant design reform movement in the last years of the 19th century and early 20th century. The appearance of furniture and decorative arts of this period was drastically altered by these new styles which swept through Europe, England and America.

Art Nouveau derives its name from a shop in Paris, "La Maison de l'Art Nouveau", which retailed glass and furniture designed by Tiffany, Lalique and Gallé. Most Art Nouveau objects are characterized by sinuous, fluid forms derived from nature often with elongated vertical proportions. In Scotland Charles Rennie Macintosh combined Art Nouveau proportions, and the straight lines of the Arts and Crafts movement, with modern ideas of furniture as art and sculpture.

Art Deco embraces two very different approaches to applied arts. On the one hand, designers made objects of the highest quality; on the other, they developed clean simple shapes suitable for mass production.

In the middle years of the 20th century Arts and Crafts, Art Nouveau and Art Deco became unfashionable, but today almost any object reflecting these styles is collectible and prices for many small, mass produced objects are still relatively low.

FURNITURE

Art Nouveau and Art Deco furniture cover a wide spectrum of quality and prices. The most sought-after and valuable pieces are large, commissioned, hand-made items, by known designers. Smaller functional objects, such as writing desks, chairs and original mass-produced furniture, are widely available and relatively inexpensive.

► **CHARLES RENNIE MACKINTOSH**
The most influential British designer at the turn of the century, Charles Rennie Mackintosh generally designed his furniture on commission. The clean simple lines of this chair are in stark contrast to the fluid forms of French Art Nouveau furniture. A similar chair estimated to sell for $40,000-60,000 fetched $460,000 in 1994.

◄ **LIBERTY**
Furniture made for the influential firm of Liberty & Co. is usually marked with a Liberty label and though highly collectible is affordable. This dressing table is part of a set which also includes two wardrobes; the suite would be worth $6,000.

▼ EMILE GALLÉ

This small table, designed by Emile Gallé, one of the leading French exponents of the Art Nouveau style, has five features characteristic of most Gallé furniture:

● strong sculptural quality
● inventive design
● fruitwood marquetry inlay
● stylized floral decorative motifs
● a signature.

$25,000+. A similar table belonging to entertainer Barbara Streisand estimated to sell for $25,000-35,000 sold for $48,000 in 1994.

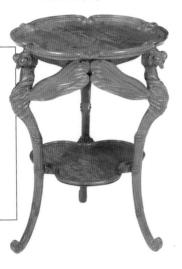

BEWARE

Later mass produced pieces marked GALLÉ lack the originality and quality of handmade items made for exhibitions and are therefore less valuable.

WHAT TO LOOK FOR

Much unsigned furniture of the 1920s and 30s, such as this cocktail cabinet, remains relatively inexpensive. Quality can vary, you should look for:

● uncracked veneers
● original upholstery
● pale woods
● dramatic but simple geometric forms. $1,000+

LUDWIG MIES VAN DER ROHE

One of van der Rohe's most popular designs, the Barcelona chair, was first made in 1929 and has been mass-produced continuously since the Second World War. Pre-mass-production chairs are very rare, worth around $100,000. Later versions, $1,000–2,000. Prewar:

● a bent chrome steel frame of separate sections joined by lap joints and screwed with chrome-headed bolts

Postwar:

● a continuous bent chromed steel frame; no screws.

GLASS

Unlike most earlier glass (see p98-103), the value of a piece of Art Nouveau or Art Deco glassware is dependent largely on its maker or designer. This was the heyday of influential glass makers such as Emile Gallé, Daum and Lalique in France, and Louis Comfort Tiffany in America. Designers no longer tailor-made their output of glassware primarily for the dining-table. Glass was increasingly used to make a plethora of decorative vases and lamps and, spurred on by the new requirements of "modern" life, designers produced objects as diverse as car mascots, jewelry and scent bottles. All named glass is widely collected, and the best pieces are very expensive, but you can still find unmarked pieces or smaller objects for relatively modest prices.

◀ DAUM FRÈRES
Daum glass, such as this vase, is often very similar to that made by Gallé but can usually be identified by a gilt signature *DAUM NANCY* in black enamel on the underside. $3,000

◀ GALLÉ GLASS
The best pieces, such as this lamp, are made from hand-carved cameo glass (formed by fusing two or more layers of colored glass, the top layer carved to reveal the colors underneath). Later machine-made versions are less valuable and are identifiable because the carving is not so deeply cut. $15,000+

FAKES
Fake Art Nouveau glassware abounds – among the objects most likely to deceive are:
● "Tiffany" lamps – with fake marks – identifiable because they do not usually have the marked pad on the shade.
● Cameo glass marked "Gallé" – recognizable by its stiff, lifeless decoration.

MARKS
Gallé pieces are usually marked with a cameo or incise-carved signature. If you see a star after the signature, the piece was made during the first three years after Gallé's death, between 1904-1907.

▶ TIFFANY
Tiffany lamps have bronze or gilt bronze bases and leaded glass shades. The bases and shades were interchangeable. Designs were floral and geometric. This laburnum lamp, $30,000-80,000+

LALIQUE

All types of glass made by the most famous glass designer of the Art Deco period, René Lalique, are highly collectible. His prolific output included car mascots, clocks, lighting, jewelry, furniture and figurines. Lalique's distinctive wares were also much imitated so before buying something you think is by Lalique ask yourself the following questions . . .

IS IT LALIQUE?

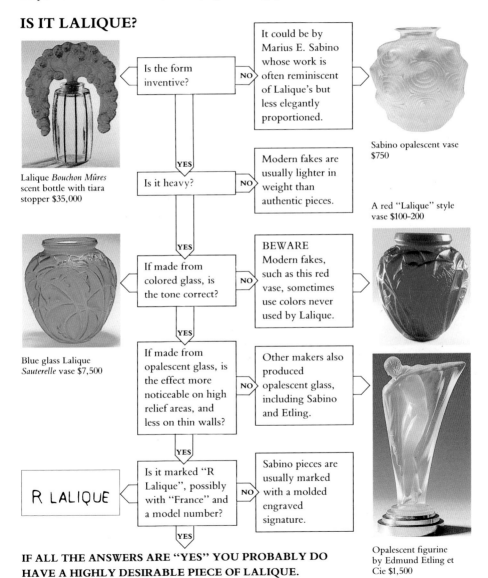

Lalique *Bouchon Mûres* scent bottle with tiara stopper $35,000

Is the form inventive? — NO → It could be by Marius E. Sabino whose work is often reminiscent of Lalique's but less elegantly proportioned.

Sabino opalescent vase $750

A red "Lalique" style vase $100–200

Is it heavy? — NO → Modern fakes are usually lighter in weight than authentic pieces.

Blue glass Lalique *Sauterelle* vase $7,500

If made from colored glass, is the tone correct? — NO → BEWARE Modern fakes, such as this red vase, sometimes use colors never used by Lalique.

If made from opalescent glass, is the effect more noticeable on high relief areas, and less on thin walls? — NO → Other makers also produced opalescent glass, including Sabino and Etling.

Is it marked "R Lalique", possibly with "France" and a model number? — NO → Sabino pieces are usually marked with a molded engraved signature.

R LALIQUE

IF ALL THE ANSWERS ARE "YES" YOU PROBABLY DO HAVE A HIGHLY DESIRABLE PIECE OF LALIQUE.

Opalescent figurine by Edmund Etling et Cie $1,500

CERAMICS

Whether you prefer the subtle sensuality of the Art Nouveau potters, or the uncluttered modern approach of the Art Deco era, pottery of this period provides something to suit almost every taste. If you're an inexperienced collector this could be an ideal category to begin with: most pottery and porcelain is marked; wares by the most famous potters are usually well documented; and many pieces are still inexpensive.

During the Art Nouveau period vases of floral and organic shapes were sometimes decorated with languid, scantily clad maidens. During the Arts and Crafts period Art Pottery was produced from the 1870s to 1920 primarily for decorative purposes and often but not always made by an individual craftsman, laying the foundation for the Studio Pottery movement which followed. In stark contrast, the clean bright motifs and machine made shapes of Art Deco pottery evoke the spirit of the jazz age.

◄ WILLIAM MOORCROFT
If you see a piece of pottery decorated with raised lines, which look as if they've been applied with an icing nozzle, the chances are it was made by William Moorcroft, at the famous Macintyre Pottery in Staffordshire. This "Iris" vase illustrates the technique, known as "tube-line", made with hand-applied fine lines of slip. $700–1,000

▲ ROYAL COPENHAGEN
The serpentine movement of this group, and the soft pastel shades in which it's decorated, identify this as a typical piece of Royal Copenhagen porcelain. The group, known as "The Rock and the Wave", is so popular it is still reproduced today. Dating can be tricky but different marks were used and these can give a clue as to when the piece was made. $1,000–1,200

► DOULTON & CO
This factory produced such a wide variety of wares that many buyers collect nothing else! You'll have to pay more if a piece of Doulton was made by a famous designer. This vase was decorated by the prominent designer Mark V. Marshall, and would be worth over $7,500 in England, less in the US; a piece by a less prestigious designer might be worth a tenth as much.

| 1894–1900 | 1894–1922 | from 1905 |

CLARICE CLIFF

The most famous British Art Deco pottery was designed by Clarice Cliff who produced such a variety of shapes and patterns that auction sales are devoted entirely to her wares. Prices depend on pattern, rarity and condition. Crocus and Gay Day are among the most common and affordable.

Although produced in large quantities, all genuine Clarice Cliff, was hand-painted and you should be able to see brush strokes in the colored enamels.

FUTURISTIC SHAPES, EXEMPLIFIED BY THIS *c.*1935 TEAPOT ARE TYPICAL OF CLARICE CLIFF'S ADVENTUROUS POTTERY. $700-1,200

Condition is of paramount importance to value and restoration can be difficult to spot. Check spouts and handles for signs of chipping and run a finger around rims and bases to see if they're intact.

The warm yellow "honey glaze" gives the background an ivory color seen on many Clarice Cliff wares.

Most pieces are marked with a printed mark and facsimile signature.

Decoration is sometimes outlined in black.

BEWARE OF FAKES

Reproductions and fakes can usually be distinguished by their inferior color and design. This jug looks washed out compared with the vibrant colors on the teapot, and the handle is too thin.

DESIRABLE DESIGNS

- *Age of Jazz* figures
- Blue glaze *Inspiration* pattern
- *Circus* series – designed by Dame Laura Knight
- Geometric designs
- Rare patterns are *Carpet, Latona, Night* and *Day.*

SCULPTURE

As sculpture, which had hitherto been rather expensive, enjoyed an upsurge of popularity in the early 20th century, inexpensive small-scale figures epitomizing the Art Nouveau and Deco styles became widely available. The female form is a recurring subject; Art Nouveau sculpture shows women in dreamy poses, or draped across functional objects such as lamps. Sculpture of the Art Deco era reflects the roaring twenties, depicting elegant ladies playing golf, dancing and smoking.

◀ GUSTAV GURSCHNER
Form, function and decoration are typically intermingled in this bizarre *c.*1900 bronze nautilus shell lamp by Bavarian sculptor, Gustav Gurschner. Similar fluid shapes were favored by French sculptors; English pieces are usually less stylized. $5,000

▶ FERDINAND PREISS
The most valuable Art Deco sculptures are usually those made from "chryselephantine" – a combination of bronze and ivory. This one dates from the 1930s and was made by Ferdinand Preiss, one of the most famous sculptors of such figures. $6,000

▲ DEMÈTRE CHIPARUS
The bases of Art Deco sculptures are integral to the composition and can help identify the maker. The architectural quality of the base of this figure is typical of Chiparus. $9,000-12,000+.

SCULPTURE CARE
The patination of a bronze is fundamental to its appeal. **Never** polish a bronze or you will seriously reduce its value.

POSTERS

The growth of the Art Nouveau movement coincided with the development of increasingly versatile lithographic printing techniques. Prominent artists such as Alphonse Mucha, Jules Chéret and Adolphe J. M. Cassandre exploited the media with unrivalled originality. Advertising posters were produced in prolific quantities and nowadays these are keenly collected. The designer, aesthetic appeal, and condition of a poster, will all influence value.

PRINTING TECHNIQUES

ENGRAVING – design incised on copperplate with burin, inked and printed.

ETCHING – copperplate coated with wax into which design is drawn, an acid bath bites design into plate, inked and printed.

LITHOGRAPH – design drawn on stone with a greasy pencil, dampened and inked; paper and stone go through press together.

PHOTOGRAVURE – photographic negative applied to copper plate, inked and printed.

▼ ALPHONSE MUCHA
Mucha's posters usually combine a romanticized female figure with draped and floral details.
$10,000–15,000

IS IT OLD?
Art Nouveau and Art Deco Posters have been reproduced in recent years; reproductions are identifiable by:
● thicker, usually glossy modern paper
● color printing made up of tiny dots you can see with a magnifying glass – authentic lithographs have flat areas of color.

▲ JULES CHÉRET
Many posters were printed on cheap paper and have suffered from foxing, tearing, fading or staining. Avoid those that are badly damaged or glued to a backboard. This Chéret poster is in unusually good condition. $1,200+

▲ J. M. CASSANDRE
Art Deco posters are usually strikingly simple and focus on a single dominant image, with strong emphasis on lettering. This poster for the liner *Normandie* is the most valuable of the posters designed by the famous French artist Cassandre. $9,000+

Although many old textiles are too delicate to use for their original purposes, you can often treat them as you would a picture and hang them on your walls – and this is one reason why in recent years textiles have enjoyed a huge increase in popularity.

Because of their inherent fragility, age and condition are fundamental to the value of all antique textiles. Among the earliest and most valuable English textiles are stumpwork pictures made in the 17th century. These raised, embroidered pictures often contain amusing inconsistencies of scale – figures may be dwarfed by gigantic insects, huge flowers loom over tiny houses – but this is part of their naive charm. American samplers are worked on linen with silk and linen threads.

Textiles made in the 19th century and early 20th century tend to be widely available and far less expensive. Those made in the Middle East, China, Japan and India are often especially colorful. European tapestries of this period sometimes imitate earlier styles, but with a brighter range of colors. If a whole tapestry is beyond your budget you could buy a small fragment or a chair cover and make a cushion from it. There is also an abundance of samplers, shawls and lace from which to choose.

EMBROIDERY

Throughout the centuries sewing was an essential skill for women and part of every young girl's education. Some school girl embroideries served as a visual recipe book of different stitches. In general the finer the stitching, the brighter the colors, and the more visually arresting, the more desirable the piece. Silk embroideries are generally more valuable than those sewn in wool. It is best to avoid badly damaged textiles, unless they are particularly unusual.

▲ **STUMPWORK** Stumpwork embroidery incorporates distinctive areas of raised decoration, formed by padding certain areas of the design. Even though this *c.*1660 stumpwork picture has had some restoration to the ivory silk background, it would still be worth $2,500-5,000 for small one, $12,000-15,000 larger ones.

SAMPLER CARE
- Hang samplers away from strong sunlight to avoid fading.
- If storing English samplers make sure they are well protected from moths; use plenty of moth balls, but never let them touch the wool.

▼ SUSANIS

According to legend, embroidered *Susanis* (the word means stitch or needle in Persian), such as this one from Bokhara, were stitched by young girls before they were married. They were used as a covering for the bridal bed and ripped in half when the bride lost her virginity! $1,200-2,500

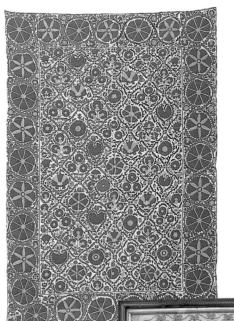

▲ BERLIN WOOLWORK

Berlin woolwork pictures such as this, were made in large numbers in the mid-19th century. Subjects vary enormously and can affect price. This one shows a scene taken from a Sir Walter Scott novel and is worth about $350-500. Pictures of birds and dogs are always popular and can cost $600-1,000.

▶ SAMPLERS

Typically this sampler contains the name of the maker – Mary Read – and the date – 1838. $800-1,200. American samplers are less symmetrical, have larger pictorial elements, freer designs, and less verse. $1,500-2,500+

WHAT TO LOOK FOR

● Desirable subjects such as: houses, people, birds, insects and flowers in appealing arrangements.
● Needlework pictures worked in silk and watercolor; mourning pictures; names, dates, and places are a bonus.
● Reasonable condition – avoid 19th century samplers if they're badly damaged or have holes.

WOVEN TEXTILES

In draughty 17th and 18th century interiors, tapestry hangings provided an essential source of warmth. It was only as wallpaper became popular, and houses warmer, that tapestries dwindled in popularity. Nowadays, although no longer essential, tapestries have once again become fashionable, and collectible. Not all are prohibitively expensive; you can find small snippets of

◀ TAPESTRY
This 19th century Beauvais tapestry is so finely woven that you could easily mistake it for an oil painting – a sign that it's of the highest quality. The elaborate border is copied from picture frames of the period and the design is after a painting by the 18th century artist François Boucher.
$15,000

◀ TAPESTRY CUSHIONS
Tapestry cushions are often fragments of a larger piece; this one uses 17th century tapestry which was probably once part of the border of a large panel. Like most cushions of this type, it's mounted on fabric of a much later date.
$750–1,200+

WHAT TO LOOK FOR
- rich dark colors, predominantly reds and oranges, gold, turquoise, green and black.
- heavy, rich, soft woolen cloth enriched with silk
- complex designs inspired by Indian motifs
- generous size – 107 × 57in is average, some measure more than 150 × 76in.

▶ PAISLEY SHAWLS
Paisley shawls such as this became popular because the voluminous skirts fashionable in the mid-19th century made it impossible to wear coats! Named after a town in Scotland, these shawls were also produced in England and France, and developed from an Indian design.
$600+

flowery Aubusson, or finely woven Beauvais tapestry for quite modest sums. Look out for door hangings (*portières*) and seat covers, or fragments of large tapestries, as these are often surprisingly inexpensive.

If the grandeur of tapestry is too overpowering for your taste you might find the homely charm of an antique quilt or the delicacy of antique lace more appealing.

Quilts usually date from the 19th and early 20th century and have become popular with collectors in America, where many of the finest were made.

Most lace seen today is machine-made, and dates from the late 18th century onwards. Hand-made lace has an appealing irregularity in its appearance, and early pieces are particularly valuable.

▶ **LOOKING AFTER LACE**
- Early lace, such as this 18th-century flounce, was usually made from linen, a robust fibre, so pieces can be framed and hung on a wall.
- Never display lace by pinning it – rust stains are very difficult to remove.
- Store lace between sheets of acid free tissue paper. $3,500

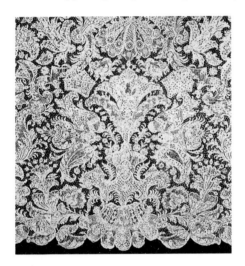

▼ **DATING A QUILT**
Newspaper or scrap paper templates were often used to stiffen the fabric patches in old quilts such as this American one. You might find laundry lists, letters, or news stories – and these can indicate the date and maker of the quilt. $3,000-5,000

Dolls have been played with and treasured by children both rich and poor from the earliest times, to the present day. Most dolls are categorized by collectors according to the medium of the head (which is often different from that of the body). Among the most valuable are those made from wood in the 18th century and from bisque in the 19th century; both types can fetch several thousand dollars at auction. But you don't have to spend a fortune to build up an interesting collection of dolls. Composition (a substance similar to *papier mâché*), wax over composition and fabric dolls are far less expensive.

Clothes may add to the value of any doll. Some had extremely elaborate wardrobes and those in their original costumes command a premium. However, don't ignore badly dressed or even naked dolls. If your doll hasn't a thing to wear, one way of boosting her value is to buy her a new outfit!

Teddy bears are a relatively recent addition to the collector's market. The jointed bear was only invented at the turn of the 20th century. The most sought-after bears are those made by Steiff, the premier maker of German bears. English bears of the 1930s and later tend to be more affordable.

DOLL TYPES

During the 19th and 20th centuries many new doll-making techniques evolved; materials as varied as *papier mâché*, parian, rag, celluloid, wax, plastic and vinyl were used for doll-making. Because the range is so extensive, collectors often focus their collections on dolls of a particular type. The table below highlights four categories. By no means all the dolls featured are very old or priceless – as you can see, even a Barbie or a Sindy can be collectible!

Bisque dolls are the largest group of collector's dolls and are covered on the following two pages.

HEAD TYPES

Dolls are classified according to their head type; these illustrations show some of the most common types:

Shoulder head

Swivel head

Open head

Solid domed head

POURED WAX	WAX OVER COMPOSITION	FABRIC	VINYL	
A Madame Montinari poured wax doll 20-22in, $800-1,000+	A Pumpkin head doll 22-25in, $475-525	A Lenci pressed felt doll 16-18in, $1,200+	A Pair of c.1960s Barbies $600-700 (boxed)	
• hollow wax head and shoulders in one piece • stiff muslin or fabric body • closed mouth • inserted eyes and hair • wax arms and legs	• large hollow molded head made from *papier mâché* dipped in wax and painted • pupilless eyes • wood, cloth or *papier-mâché* body • turned wooden legs and arms	• molded fabric head and stuffed fabric body • painted or stitched facial features • hair made from wool, cotton or mohair or painted on	• hollow soft vinyl head • rooted hair • jointed limbs • painted or inserted eyes • registered trademark on head or body	IDENTIFYING FEATURES
• dolls by famous makers, especially Pierotti, Montinari and John Edwards • softly modelled features • glass eyes • well defined fingers and toes	• good condition – these dolls aren't rare so damage is not acceptable • real hair; molded bonnets – rare but desirable • original, colorful, elaborate clothes	• dolls by famous makers such as Kathe Kruse, Lenci, Steiff • expressive features, sideways glancing eyes • good condition – felt dolls are vulnerable to moths • elaborate clothes with original labels	• Barbies with holes in the feet– these are the earliest • Barbies with titian or brunette hair • dolls from the 60s with designer-inspired wardrobes • dolls with original packaging • black Francies	WHAT TO LOOK FOR

BISQUE DOLLS

Bisque dolls, with heads made from un-glazed, tinted porcelain, are among the most elaborate and valuable of all collectors' dolls. The finest French bisques, made by leading makers such as Jumeau, Bru, Gaultier and Steiner, were expensive status symbols even when first made, and remained very much the province of pampered children from the most affluent homes. The earliest French bisques resembled fashionable ladies and came equipped with wardrobes of elaborate, fashionable clothes. Later in the century, the firm of Jumeau began making dolls with child-like features, large eyes and chubby bodies known as bébés – these soon became enormously popular, and although German manufacturers followed suit and produced their own child dolls they could never quite match the quality of the French bébé. German manufacturers eventually recovered the lion's share of the market in the early 20th century, when they introduced realistic "character" dolls, with crying, laughing, frowning and smiling faces.

The price of bisque dolls ranges from a hundred to several thousand dollars and depends on the maker, condition and quality, and on details such as the rarity of the mold number (found on the back of the head) as well as the type of mouth (closed is better than open), eyes and body.

▼ **GAULTIER FASHION DOLL**
Fashion dolls can be dated by the shape of their bodies, which were made to fit the costumes of the day. This François Gaultier doll has a narrow waist and broad hips and shoulders well-suited to her bustle dress – which was fashionable c.1870.
$2,000–4,000

◀ **JUMEAU DOLL**
The *crême de la crême* of collector's dolls, Jumeaus, such as this bébé, are worth as much as $4,000–7,000+. You can recognize a Jumeau by its pale-colored bisque and large glass eyes.
Many bisque-headed dolls have composition bodies and limbs which are prone to damage (detail left). Slight wear is acceptable and you should only repaint a doll as a last resort.

GERMAN CHARACTER DOLLS

THIS BISQUE-HEADED DOLL, MADE BY ERNST HEUBACH C.1914, HAS AN EXPRESSIVE FACE TYPICAL OF GERMAN CHARACTER DOLLS. SHE IS OF MEDIUM QUALITY AND WOULD BE WORTH $200-600

This body is known as a "five piece bent limb" body, because the arms and legs are realistically bent.

The value is reduced because the doll has a replacement wig – original wigs are preferable.

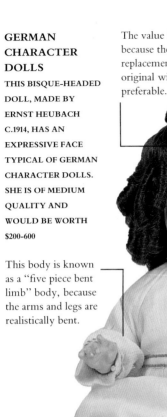

OTHER MARKS TO LOOK FOR

S I5 H
939
Simon & Halbig
(active c.1869-1930)

HEU·BACH
Gerbruder Heubach
(active 1820-1945)

Made in Germany
Armand Marseille.
Armand Marseille
(active 1885-1930)

J.D.K.
Made in 13 Germany
Kestner & Co
(active 1816-1930)

Most bisque dolls have hand–painted eyebrows – delicately feathered brows like this are a sign of quality.

Open mouths were introduced in c.1900. Although more expensive at the time, nowadays dolls with closed mouths are more valuable than those with open ones.

GOOGLIE DOLLS

Some character dolls have very distinctive features and expressions. Dolls such as this, with roguish expressions, large round eyes and impish smiles, known as "Googlies" are among the most sought after character dolls. This one would be worth $4,500+.

This doll is wearing her original clothes which adds to her value. If you need to replace your doll's clothes you can sometimes find old baby clothes to fit larger dolls, or use old fabric to make suitable replacements.

TEDDY BEARS

Teddy bears have enjoyed a huge increase in popularity in recent years. The earliest bears were made by the Steiff company in Germany at the beginning of the 20th century. This well-known company was founded by Margarete Steiff who was crippled by polio and confined to a wheel chair as a child. With their pointed snouts, long arms and feet and humped backs, early Steiff bears look much more like real bears than most teddies of today, and are the most valuable of all collectors' bears.

Bears are called "Teddies" thanks to the American Ideal Toy Company. Morris Michtom, the company's founder, was inspired by a cartoon showing President Theodore Roosevelt sparing the life of a bear cub. The cartoon was so popular that bears were adopted as the President's mascot, and Michtom reputedly wrote to ask his permission to call the bears he was making "Teddy". The President agreed and bears have been known as Teddy ever since.

As bears became more and more popular they were produced by increasing numbers of toy companies on both sides of the Atlantic. In America almost 25 different companies were making teddy bears by 1907. The largest were Ideal, Aetna, and the Bruin Manufacturing Company. Heckla, Gund and Strauss also made high quality bears. In England Chad Valley, Merrythought, Dean's Rag Book, Chiltern and J.K. Farnell were major makers. Few bears were made during World War II but after the war production resumed.

The most valuable bears are early examples in good condition, made by famous makers. In general, Steiff bears remain the most valuable of all because of their high quality and appeal.

ENGLISH MAKERS

Several prominent English manufacturers of teddy bears prospered from c.1915 onwards. Most English bears were originally marked on fabric labels stitched to the foot:

◀ **CHAD VALLEY** Chad bears date from the 1920's. Early bears were made of luxuriant mohair, usually gold colored, with soft kapok stuffed limbs. $200-500

▶ **MERRYTHOUGHT** Bears were made from the 1930s; this one has large round ears and joined claws which are typical of this maker. $200-500

▼ **J.K.FARNELL & CO.** Farnells supplied teddy bears to Harrods during the 1920s. Winnie the Pooh was reputedly made by this company. The angled ears and large amber glass eyes of this c.1918 bear are typical of this maker. $300-1,000+ (for larger bears)

STEIFF BEARS

THIS c.1908 BEAR IS
THE MOST COMMON
TYPE OF STEIFF BEAR.
THE HUMPED BACK IS
TYPICAL OF EARLY
STEIFFS. LATER BEARS
HAVE LESS
PROMINENT HUMPS.
$1,000+ (DEPENDING
ON SIZE)

BEWARE

Early Steiff and
American bears had
shoe button eyes
sewn on. English
bears have glass eyes
attached with wire
which can come
loose, so keep out of
reach of children.

Steiff bears have a
distinctive button in
the left ear. Early
buttons had an
elephant logo or were
plain. Later ones had
the word *"Steiff"* prin-
ted; after 1950 "Steiff"
appears in script.

The long curved
limbs and large oval
felt paws with
narrow wrists and
ankles are
characteristic of Steiff
bears.

BEAR CARE

- Holes can be mended without reducing value but use
  similar fabric for patches.
- Dirty bears need specialist
  cleaning; untreated dirt
  makes the fabric rot.
  - Put new additions in a
    plastic bag with moth-
    balls over night to kill
    any infestation.

Paw pads are usually
made from felt and
are especially prone
to wear; this bear has
replacement pads,
which will affect its
value.

Most bears are made
from beige or gold
mohair plush.
Unusual colors are
more desirable. Steiff
also made some bears
in red, black, apricot
and white mohair.

AMERICAN BEARS

American bears, like this, have
distinctive football-shaped bodies, large
humps, narrow arms and legs
and small feet. $400+; 18in or
more, $1,000+

If you are thinking of beginning a collection of toys there is a huge range of prices and varieties from which to choose. Many collectors specialize in a particular area, such as clockwork toys, robots or cars, or in a particular maker. You need to be sure of your area of interest before visiting the larger auction houses because many sell different types of toys – such as soldiers, model cars or trains – in specialty sales.

Prices for toys depend on the maker, the rarity of the model and the condition. Although chips and dents are virtually inevitable, a toy in mint condition, or with its original packaging is what every serious collector longs for. Repainting will nearly always reduce the value of a collector's toy so only repaint items as a last resort.

Toys made by well-known firms are always sought after, and minor damage is acceptable if the toy is made by a premier firm such as Bing, Märklin or Lehmann. Viewing sales and visiting specialist dealers is the best way of getting to know which models are the most desirable. Once you have a good feel for prices, you don't have to buy from an upmarket auction house or dealer. Because many collectible toys are not very old it's always worth scouring the local thrift shop or garage sale for bargains!

WOOD, LEAD &

Less sophisticated than toys made from other substances, carved wooden toys have an appealing naïvety. Wooden toys were produced in quantity by German makers during the 18th and 19th centuries and some very collectible wooden toys were also made in America by the Schoenhut Co.

Lead became popular as a medium for various types of soldiers and other toys during the late 19th century. In Germany, France and England high quality solid and hollow-cast lead soldiers were produced by firms such as Lucotte, Heyde and William Britain and today these are among the most valuable of all toy soldiers.

Die-cast toys were also made by hollow casting and were first produced in France in c.1910. In England, Dinky Toys, part of the Meccano Co., dominated the market for die-cast toys from the 1930s-60s and rare Dinky advertising vans or unusual series are well worth looking for.

DIE-CAST TOYS
Complete sets of die-cast toys are always desirable, especially when they come with their original packaging. Although this c.1937 box is battered it still doubles the value of the set of aeroplanes. $800-1,000

DIE-CAST TOYS

▶ WOODEN TOYS
Noah's Ark was a popular subject for German wooden toy-makers. Value depends on size, quality and the number of animals; this 19th century one is large (27in wide), fairly elaborate and contains over 200 well carved animals, so it would be worth $3,000-5,000; smaller, less elaborate flat bottomed arks cost from $200.

▼ VALUE
Many 20th century wooden toys are still affordably priced. This 1930s apple filled with skittles is worth $75-100, much more if large.

▼ TOY SOLDIERS
Britain's are among the most sought after collectors' soldiers and were made using the hollow-casting method. A hollow-cast figure will have a small hole where the excess molten metal was poured out of the mold when it was made. Large set of horsemen $2,500-3,500

TINPLATE, TRAINS & CELLULOID

Horse-drawn carriages, boats, submarines, cars and even airships are just some of the many tinplate toys made during the late 19th and early 20th century which reflect contemporary developments in transportation. German toy companies led the field in the manufacture of tinplate toys and those made by well-known firms such as Bing, Märklin and Lehmann are famous for their accuracy. Trains were one of the most important forms of transportation from the mid-19th century and not surprisingly trains provided

▶ BING
This c.1906 Bing rear entry Tonneau with a clockwork mechanism is especially desirable because the high quality hand-enamelled paintwork is in near perfect condition. $7,000–8,000

◀ MÄRKLIN
Märklin toys, such as this spirit-fired torpedo boat, can be identified by their distinctive maker's mark, which in this case is stamped on the boat's rudder. $7,000–8,000

▲ TRAINS
The most valuable Märklin toys, made between 1895 and 1914, are nowadays well out of the price range of the average schoolboy. The company produced the first trains to use a numerical gauge system, to identify the differently-sized models available. This Gauge III engine, made c.1909, is the second largest size made and would be worth $20,000.

toy makers with a fertile source of inspiration. The earliest toy trains were clockwork or made from wood but by c.1900 electric trains – the dream of every school boy ever since – began to be produced in substantial numbers.

Celluloid toys were made from the late 19th century. This substance became obsolete with the advent of plastics in the 20th century and nowadays celluloid toys are keenly collected although generally less expensive than tinplate toys of a similar date.

DISNEY TOYS

The earliest tin plate Disney toys were made in Spain in 1930 and in Germany in 1931 for the British market. This German clockwork barrel organ with a thin, rather gloomy-looking Mickey is valuable. Even though he's lost his tail, Minnie has been repainted, and there are signs of rusting, it would sell for $2,500-4,000; mint in its original box, $20,000

WHAT TO LOOK FOR

- Mickey and Minnie dolls by Steiff, Dean's, Knickerbocker, Charlotte Clark
- Mickey Mouse china tea sets
- Celluloid Donald Ducks with long bill c.1935
- Earliest Mickeys have five fingers and teeth showing.

◀ LICENSING
The box of this celluloid Mickey on Pluto, says "Made in Occupied Japan Copyright Walt Disney Prod." It was made in 1946-48 under a special licence. Licensed toys are more desirable than unauthorized ones. $3,500-6,000

CELLULOID
Celluloid toys are highly flammable and easily damaged. Be wary: brush strokes from liquid plastic indicate a fake. Fake laser printed boxes have stripes under magnification.

Rock and pop memorabilia is one of the newest, most exciting and accessibly priced collecting areas – although it does have its high prices too. The record is $2.3 million paid for John Lennon's Rolls Royce in 1985.

Almost any object in some way connected with a well-known star can be collectible; even tickets, posters and other printed ephemera made for concerts and tours are saleable. The most sought-after pieces are those closely linked with the stars themselves. Collectors pay especially high prices for the musical instruments with which a star is associated; electric guitars can fetch several thousands dollars if they were played at a memorable concert.

Clothes are another popular collecting area. The most valuable garments are those recognizably linked with the image of their owner. Perhaps they were photographed wearing them, or used them at an important concert, or in a video. Elton John's wacky shoes, Madonna's gold leather corset, Michael Jackson's rhinestone-studded glove have all attracted huge media attention and prices to match when they've come under the hammer. But not all collectible clothes are prohibitively expensive – prices for a roadie's jacket, or a T-Shirt sporting the name and logo of a tour or album start at less than $100.

THE 50S & 60S

The golden era of rock and roll is not surprisingly the focus for many collectors' attentions. Memorabilia from this period is relatively scarce compared with that of the following decades so even printed concert programs and magazines, which were made in their thousands, and once cost under $2, are keenly collected. The most desirable memorabilia relates to the big names of the period whose popularity endures today. Among the most popular are Elvis Presley, Buddy Holly, Bill Haley and Bob Dylan – to name but a few.

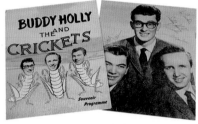

▲ **BUDDY HOLLY**
Buddy Holly continues to enjoy a following so memorabilia relating to his career attracts high prices. This signed souvenir program marks his group's only tour to England. $1,000

▲ **JIM MORRISON**
Jim Morrison has always been collectible but his popularity enjoyed an upsurge with the release of Oliver Stone's film charting his life. These working lyrics for *The Celebration of the Lizard* give a revealing glimpse of Morrison's creative process and are worth $6,000-9,000.

BEATLES MEMORABILIA

The Beatles have a unique place in the history of pop music: no previous group had enjoyed such success and they pioneered the vibrant new pop music which epitomized the sounds of the 1960s. Although Beatles memorabilia comes up for sale quite regularly, almost any object which celebrates their fame is of interest to collectors.

▲ BEATLES DOLLS
The wide range of commercial Beatles merchandise made during the 1960s and 70s reflects the group's phenomenal popularity. Among the diverse Beatles

objects are lamps, scrap books, wigs and stockings. These plastic Beatles dolls, dressed in Sgt. Pepper's Lonely Hearts Club Band costumes, cost around $200.

▶ LENNON DRAWINGS
This hand-drawn Christmas card was given to Cynthia Powell by John Lennon in 1958 and encloses a revealing eight page letter to

Cynthia, whom he married five years later. Drawings by John Lennon are among the most desirable pieces of Beatles memorabilia and can fetch very high prices. $10,000

▶ RINGO DRUM SET
Although this drum set is a toy it would attract collectors because it is rare to find these in near perfect condition, complete with stand, sticks, original box and instructions. $300–400

WHAT TO LOOK FOR
● Hand written lyrics to popular songs
● Autographed letters
● Autographed photographs
● Artwork for record sleeves
● Animation cels from *Yellow Submarine* ($400–600).

THE 70S

The 70s marked the heyday of rock star rebels such as The Sex Pistols, David Bowie, Marc Bolan and Bruce Springsteen whose new approach to rock music was to have a profound influence on musicians of the following generations. Because of its nostalgic appeal, memorabilia of the 70s is widely collected, although pieces usually fetch less meteoric prices than the items which relate to the superstars of today.

▼ PETE TOWNSHEND
The fact that this guitar is smashed paradoxically adds to its value because it highlights its original owner's "bad boy" image. It's accompanied by a letter which details the guitar's history: *"... I broke it in 1973 in a rage of frustration in my studio..."* $6,000–9,000.

▲ WOODSTOCK
Posters relating to important concerts are among the most affordable pieces of rock and pop memorabilia. The concerts held in Woodstock, New York in August 1969, and on the Isle of Wight, England in 1969 and 1970 were key events and attracted audiences of over a quarter of a million. Promotional posters for these concerts are worth around $100–200.

◀ ELTON JOHN
Elton John was one of the first stars to exploit the possibilities of stage costume. Extraordinary glasses and flamboyant shoes such as these became his trademark and are eagerly collected. $1,000–2,000 (a pair)

THE 80S & 90S

The advent of the pop video was largely responsible for the increased importance stars of the 80s and 90s attached to their appearance and image. As concerts and tours became increasingly sophisticated, the star's visual impact became as important as the music. Costumes, often made by leading designers, are an obvious way of establishing the star's persona. Hence, outfits of increasingly extravagant design, have become the symbol of many of the most famous celebrities of the past two decades.

▶ PRINCE

All Prince's clothes are specially made for him and because his swashbuckling outfits are fundamental to his on-stage image those that come up for sale are very desirable. This suit made from turquoise and blue silk was sold with a letter of authentication stating where it was made and confirming that it was worn at the 1988 Grammy Awards by Prince. $7,500. His shoes brought $3,100 in 1993.

TOP FIVE COLLECTIBLE STARS

- **Madonna** Changes her image for each tour so anything directly connected with one of her "looks" will be very desirable.
- **Prince** Neo-romantic clothes always sought after.
- **Elton John** Shoes, glasses, hats – the more zany the higher the price.
- **Queen** Anything connected with Freddy Mercury.
- **Michael Jackson** Almost anything is collectible.

▲ MICHAEL JACKSON

Michael Jackson was often photographed wearing this rhinestone-studded glove which was perhaps the most instantly recognizable piece of Rock and Pop clothing of the decade. The glove sold in 1991 for nearly $30,000; a record for any piece of Michael Jackson costume!

PRESENTATION DISCS

The most valuable awards are the gold and platinum discs presented by the record company to the star. Gold discs are given for over 500,000 albums, or 1 million singles sold; platinum discs are given for over 1 million albums or 2 million singles sold. This silver presentation disc for Madonna's *You Can Dance* is worth $700+.

Whether because of their historical interest, high-quality craftsmanship, or because they are such potent reminders of the heroics of the past, the relics of war have long fascinated collectors. The terms "Arms and Militaria" cover a surprisingly wide range of objects and include armor, firearms, edged weapons, medals, badges, uniforms, and even prints and cigarette cards.

Armor has been made, in one form or another, from the dawn of civilization to the 19th century; but most pieces commonly seen on the market today date from the 16th century onwards. Full sets of armor are extremely valuable and if you're a novice collector you must learn to recognize the numerous "marriages" between pieces from different periods. So long as you realize the set is a composite and this fact is allowed for in the price, marriages are acceptable.

Antique firearms are often more accessibly priced. A 19th century flintlock pistol could cost $300 or less; 18th century examples are priced from about $1,000. Before you start buying, remember to check legal restrictions which are always changing. American arms and accoutrements are more in demand here than European pieces which are low priced in the US compared to their country of origin.

EDGED WEAPONS

Edged weapons, which include swords, sabers, dirks and bayonets, come up for sale frequently and, depending on the type of weapon you choose, it is possible to build up a collection for relatively little outlay. Most antique firearms fall into one of two categories: flintlocks, which use a flint to make a spark and ignite the charge; or percussion guns, in which a metal cap containing a small explosive charge is ignited by the stroke of the hammer. Pennsylvania long rifles and their accoutrements are an art form. A flint lock long rifle with carved and engraved brass decorations is worth $5,000+. Confederate fire arms are rare and expensive.

◄ LONG ARMS
Unusual early weapons always command a premium. This German wheel-lock sporting rifle, dated 1666, has several quality features which make it particularly desirable:
● high quality engraving on the lock plate
● maker's mark
● elaborately inlaid stock decorated with stag horn, silver wire and mother-of-pearl. $4,000-7,000+

SWORD CARE
● wipe blades clean after handling
● wax blades after cleaning
● clean rust spots by rubbing them with a copper coin.

& ANTIQUE FIREARMS

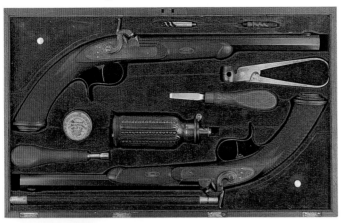

◀ DUELLING PISTOLS
In cased sets of pistols always check that all the pieces belong together and have not been added. This pair of American percussion duelling pistols comes with a range of accessories including Eley caps, and balls. $2,500-4,000. More if by certain makers.

◀ SWORDS AND DIRKS
The less than perfect condition and evidence of honest wear you can see on this set of mid-19th century Scottish regimental swords are a good sign that the set is authentic. $1,000-1,500. More with an American association (such as used in the Revolutionary War).
● The small dagger in the center is a Scottish dirk used by Scottish Highlanders.

BEWARE
● Fake engraving is sometimes added to swords to increase their value – be suspicious of harsh bright edges, and expect there to be signs of aging, such as dirt and grease between the lines.
● When fake engraving is added to a piece which already has some decoration it will often be of a different depth from the original and the background color will be different.

▼ DECORATION
The decoration on a sword reflects the status of its original owner and always adds to value. The blued and inlaid Napoleonic saber (top) belonged to a high-ranking cavalry officer. The 1831 British general officer's sword (below) is less ornate. top $1,000-2,000, below $200-300. Historical importance affects value.

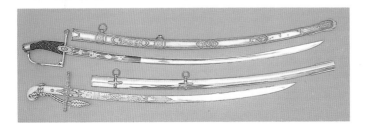

ARMOR

Swashbuckling armor from the English Civil War period (1642-49) is still fought over, but nowadays by collectors! Favorite items include "lobster-tailed" helmets, pikeman's pots (simple helmets), breast and back plates and gauntlets. Because complete suits of original armor so rarely come up for sale, even good 19th century reproductions are highly collectible and valuable. Much good quality armor of this period was made in Germany, France and Spain.

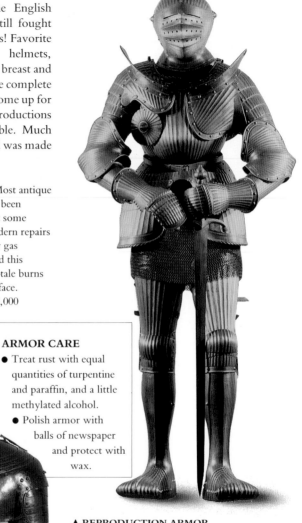

▼ CONDITION

This three-quarter Armor dates from c.1640 and was made for a Cuirassier (horseman). It is in unusually fine condition and even has its original buckles. Most antique armor has been repaired at some stage. Modern repairs are usually gas welded and this leaves tell-tale burns on the surface. $12,000-15,000

ARMOR CARE

● Treat rust with equal quantities of turpentine and paraffin, and a little methylated alcohol.
● Polish armor with balls of newspaper and protect with wax.

WHAT TO LOOK FOR

● Armorer's marks – add to value.
● Small dents in the breast plate – made from a pistol ball fired to test the armor's strength – a good sign of age.
● Funerary helmets – worn at funerals.

▲ REPRODUCTION ARMOR

Although 19th century armor was intended for decorative rather than practical purposes, much of it was very well-made. The quality of this 16th century-style fluted Maximilian armor, made c.1820, is reflected in the thickness of the metal used. A good quality suit will weigh as much as 58-60 pounds. $6,000-7,500

MISCELLANEOUS MILITARIA

The wide range of other collectible military antiques provides would-be collectors with huge scope. You may decide to concentrate on a particular regiment, a type of object, or on a period of military history. Complete early uniforms may be hard to find, but head-dresses, badges, fastenings, medals, powder flasks, postcards and prints are readily available and can form fascinating and highly decorative collections.

▶ BADGES
Whether made from metal or fabric badges are increasingly popular with collectors. Officer's head-dress badges are larger than most others and particularly sought after. Revolutionary War insignia, Civil War accoutrement plates and German World War II insignia are more popular than early 19th century British regimental badges which sell for $50-100.

▶ MEDALS
Before buying a medal check the soldier's and regiment's history to make sure he was entitled to it. This rare group was awarded to a Colonel in the Indian Army $1,000-2,000. Beware of recently engraved names of heros.

BEWARE
● Expect badges to show evidence of their age – those in perfect condition should make you suspicious.
● Fake badges usually weigh less than genuine ones and feel waxy.

▲ SHAKOS
Shakos, the cylindrical helmets, with peaks and often plumes, were popular during the 19th century. The elaborateness of their decoration can affect value. This Austro-Hungarian shako is reasonably ornate with plenty of gold trimming and is worth around $100-200. American Civil War headpieces sell for $1,500.

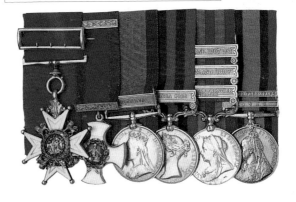

SCIENTIFIC INSTRUMENTS

However tempting it is to imagine some famous scientist of the past making a dramatic discovery with your microscope, sadly this is usually a long way from the truth. Most early scientific instruments were made either for amateur scientists, who regarded them as objects of beauty, or for professionals such as surveyors, navigators, architects and even teachers, for whom these were everyday tools of their trade.

You don't have to be knowledgeable about the history of science to appreciate the obvious skill with which scientific instruments were made. At one end of the spectrum are the machine-made precision tools

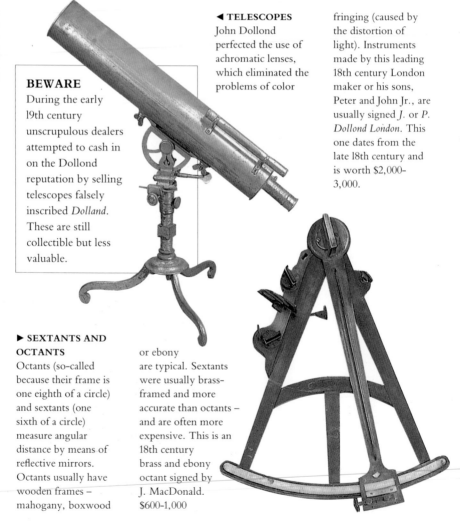

BEWARE
During the early l9th century unscrupulous dealers attempted to cash in on the Dollond reputation by selling telescopes falsely inscribed *Dolland*. These are still collectible but less valuable.

◄ TELESCOPES
John Dollond perfected the use of achromatic lenses, which eliminated the problems of color fringing (caused by the distortion of light). Instruments made by this leading 18th century London maker or his sons, Peter and John Jr., are usually signed *J.* or *P. Dollond London*. This one dates from the late 18th century and is worth $2,000-3,000.

► SEXTANTS AND OCTANTS
Octants (so-called because their frame is one eighth of a circle) and sextants (one sixth of a circle) measure angular distance by means of reflective mirrors. Octants usually have wooden frames – mahogany, boxwood or ebony are typical. Sextants were usually brass-framed and more accurate than octants – and are often more expensive. This is an 18th century brass and ebony octant signed by J. MacDonald. $600-1,000

produced during the 19th century, some of which can be bought for little over $200; at the other, are the rare, expensive examples of 18th century (and earlier) hand-crafted objects. Many instruments are ornately decorated and incorporate materials such as brass, silver, ivory and ebony. The dating of a piece can present inexperienced collectors with a problem, as the same design was often repeated over long periods. Some instruments were marked by their maker, and this usually helps with identification and dating, but also will usually increase the price. Fakes and reproductions of early instruments exist, so if in doubt always consult an expert.

> **NEVER ...** attempt to polish an old scientific instrument of any type without checking with an expert first, if you do so you may seriously damage its patina, and reduce its value dramatically.

▲ GLOBES
Terrestrial pocket globes reflect advances in mapping and circumnavigation of the world and often had cases lined with celestial globes – maps of the stars. This one was made by J. Smith in 1815. $2,500+

▼ MICROSCOPES
This Culpeper-type microscope dates from c.1730 and is one of the most desirable types of early microscope (worth $4,000-6,000). Microscopes from the 19th century are easier to find. Names to look out for are: Joseph Zentmoyer in America; Powell & Lealand, W. & S. Jones, James Powell Swift, Smith & Beck in Britain.

◀ SUNDIALS
Before watches became widely accessible and reliable, dials were often used to check the time. There are two main types of sundial: the pedestal dial, most commonly used in the garden, and the pocket dial. This typical 18th century octagonal pocket dial has an elaborately decorated brass plate and a folding gnomon (the part that casts the shadow). $500-700

CAMERAS & PHOTOGRAPHS

Although old cameras seem worlds apart from the high-tech models of today, many are still in working order and are bought to use. The earliest commercially-made cameras were produced from c.1841 and used the daguerreotype process, developed in France by L. J. M. Daguerre, in 1837. However, each daguerreotype image was unique and it was not until Henry Fox Talbot's invention of the calotype that multicopies could be produced from a single exposure. Among the most intriguing cameras are the novelty, detective and spy cameras which began to be produced as the photographic process became more refined towards the end of the century.

Unlike many other collectibles, a camera's age is not necessarily reflected in its value – the rarity and quality of a particular model are often far more important than when it was made. Japanese cameras, which have enjoyed an upsurge in popularity recently, were mass produced in the aftermath of World War II. Their quality became widely appreciated as a result of photojournalists covering the Korean War who recognized the superior quality of Japanese lenses. Today, rare and limited edition models by companies such as Nikon or Canon can fetch very high prices.

▶ **DAGUERREOTYPES**
Daguerreotypes look like mirrors – the image is formed on silvered metal, always protected behind sealed glass. Despite their relative rarity you can still find portrait groups such as this for $50-75. An interesting view or a known sitter adds to value, which can be several thousand dollars.

◀ **PHOTOGRAPH ALBUMS**
The value of early albums is affected by the subject matter of the photos and the quality of the album. This one is made from leather and mother-of-pearl. Some were made from ivory, silver, gold or mauchline ware – wood covered with tartan-printed paper. $100-200 without photos.

WHAT TO LOOK FOR

- milestone cameras which incorporate unusual technical innovations
- early handmade brass and mahogany cameras
- unusual spy cameras
- rare models by Ernst Leitz (Leica) and Zeiss
- limited edition post World War II Japanese cameras.

▶ DETECTIVE AND SPY CAMERAS

Cameras in the form of books, watches, rings and packets of cigarettes may have been made more as curiosities than for any real espionage or skulduggery, but are none the less highly popular with today's collectors – and can fetch very high prices. This c.1895 camera looks just like a pocket watch when closed and measures only 1¾ inches in diameter. Made by an American maker, John C. Hegelein, it's worth $15,000-20,000

▲ BRASS AND MAHOGANY CAMERAS

Early mahogany and brass-bound cameras are always sought after, but this 1890 Cyclographe is especially rare because it is the first panoramic camera produced by the prominent French maker V. Damoizeau. A clockwork mechanism rotated the camera around the platform and wound the film automatically. $12,000-18,000

▶ JAPANESE CAMERAS

The quality and condition of post-war cameras has an important bearing on their price. Because this Nikon S3M is one of only 195 models made in the series, and is in nearly mint condition, it would be worth over $18,000. A similar used model would be worth about $9,000.

FILM MEMORABILIA

Although there's nothing new about the magnetic allure of the cinema, film memorabilia is one of the most recent and exciting arrivals on the collecting scene. All the glamour of the movies, from the nostalgic old films from Hollywood's golden age, to the high-tech special effect films of the 1980s and 90s, are reflected in the objects which fall into this colorful collecting category.

The major types of collectible film memorabilia are costumes, props, autographs, posters, photographs and animation cels; but almost anything associated with a parti-cular film or star can be collectible. Props associated with the key stars of cult movies tend to attract the highest prices. If a particular object immediately conjures up an important star you're on to a winner – but you'll probably have to pay for it! If you can't afford the thousands needed to buy objects such as Charlie Chaplin's bowler and cane, or Harrison Ford's whip, you can still join in the fun by collecting the more affordable types of film memorabilia available. Posters, photographs, autographs and clapperboards, are often less than $100.

▶ PHOTOGRAPHS

This portrait photograph of Marlene Dietrich dates from c.1935, and unless by a famous photographer has little value unless autographed. Autographed it is worth $125.

BEWARE

Autographs on photos are often not genuine:

- Many stars allowed their secretaries to sign photographs on their behalf.
- Sometimes the negative of the photograph was signed.
- Some photographs are stamped with the star's signature.

◀ POSTERS

Among the most desirable film posters are those from classic films of the 50s and 60s. Released in 1961, *Breakfast at Tiffany's* firmly established Audrey Hepburn as a star. This poster fetched $1,400 in 1993. Posters from less successful films from the 1960s sell for under $100.

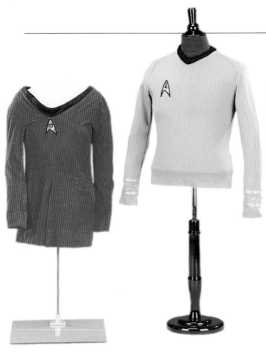

◀ STAR TREK

There is an enormous demand for *Star Trek* memorabilia. This green tunic with the famous "Enterprise" emblem, worn by William Shatner (who played Captain Kirk) in several episodes was expected to sell for $3,000–5,000 at auction – in fact it fetched $18,400!

▼ PROPS

This wooden sled stamped with the word "rosebud" was used in the film *Citizen Kane*, released in 1941. In the opening scene of the film "rosebud" is the final word spoken by the dying publishing magnate Kane. This sled fetched $60,500 in 1982.

▲ STAR WARS

The best film props are surprisingly well made and sophisticated. Darth Vadar's helmet is made from fiberglass and has see-through perspex panels in the cheek and neck areas to give better visibility during fighting sequences. $3,000+

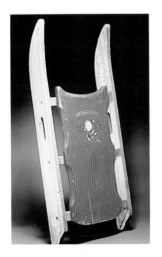

▶ CLAPPERBOARDS

Clapperboards are among the least expensive types of film memorabilia. Look for boards which come from popular films, and which are printed with the name of the production. $50+

SPORTING COLLECTIBLES

If your attic is filled with rusty old golf clubs you may be astonished to know that an old iron club recently fetched $178,400 at auction. While such a staggering price is very much the exception, there are an increasing number of collectors who bring their passion for diamond, links and river bank into their homes by collecting objects related to their favorite sport.

Prices have been boosted by the fashion for sporting decor and interior decorators have furnished elegant studies and club houses with the paraphernalia of sport.

In the not too distant past old sporting equipment was relegated to the junk shop,

nowaday you find it at upscale auctions and there are a number of dealers and auctioneers who specialize in golf, fishing or baseball.

The most sought after sporting items include objects needed to play the sport: rods, reels, clubs, rackets, gloves, bats, balls, and even uniforms worn by famous baseball players. Jerseys worn by deceased Baseball Hall of Famers have sold for $100,000; autographed baseballs start at $100 and go to $10,000 and upwards depending on player, age and condition. Trophies from all sports, as well as ceramics and printed ephemera, are very popular.

◀ GOLF
Pre-19th century golfing collectibles are extremely rare, which explains why this 18th century club made by a blacksmith reached a world record price of $178,400 in 1992.

WHAT TO LOOK FOR

- Clubs marked by one of the great makers such as Robert Forgan, Jack Morris or Hugh Philp.
- Feathery golf balls – made from hand stitched leather stuffed with dampened goose down.
- Pottery commemorating golfing events or personalities, especially if made by premier factories such as Spode and Doulton.

▲ 19TH CENTURY CLUBS
Early clubs had names rather than numbers. These are drivers, and long-nosed spoons of varying sizes. Price depends on rarity, age, quality, condition and who made it. Wood and iron clubs were made until the 1930s and can be bought for as little as $15-20. These long nosed clubs all date from c.1885 and vary in price from $1,500-3,500.

◄ **FISHING**

In England the most desirable fishing trophies are preserved behind glass in bow-fronted cases such as this bream caught in 1935. This fish might fetch a large sum in England, but much less in America where fish plaques of carved wood are preferred, selling for $4,000-6,000, or even more by a known carver.

▲ **FISHING TACKLE**

Early reels were finely made from brass, German silver, ivorene and ebonite (hard rubber simulating ebony); marked ones are particularly desirable. Look out for are Hardy Bros., Charles Farlow and S. Allcock; Meek, Milam, von Hofe and Conroy in America. Those pictured are English and worth $50-1000s. American reels by Kentucky and New York makers in the 19th century sell for $100-10,000+.

CONDITION

Reels in mint condition are rare, but those with damaged or replaced parts, or their owner's name scratched on them (unless he's famous) are best avoided.

▼ **TENNIS**

Even if he or she never won a match with it, a famous owner can transform even a modern racket into a valuable collector's item; but provenance is all-important. This Wilson racket, autographed by Jimmy Connors who used it in the 1979-81 US Open, comes with a letter of authenticity. $500-1,000

BOXES

Boxes come in a huge range of shapes, sizes and prices; some of the most exquisite ones were produced during the 18th century to contain snuff, patches or tobacco. The highest quality boxes were often made from gold or silver, and decorated with precious stones. Enamelled and porcelain boxes were also popular, some of the most attractive being made in the shape of a bird or animal. Although small 18th century boxes can cost thousands of dollars, you can still find 19th century boxes for much less. Price is usually determined by quality of the piece and the materials used. In general, boxes made from wood or *papier mâché* are widely available and most affordable.

▲ LACQUER BOXES
Lids of 19th century lacquer boxes were often decorated with a copy of a well-known Old Master painting. Erotic subjects were especially popular. This one shows nymphs bathing, with mischievous voyeurs in the bulrushes! Like many boxes of this type it was made in Germany, and is stamped on the interior *Stobwasser Fabrik*. $300–500

▼ ENAMEL BOXES
Bilston (Staffordshire), Birmingham and Battersea led the field in producing English enamel boxes during the 18th century. Chipping will reduce value; this late 18th century box is damaged around the base and is worth about $150; in better condition it might cost three times as much.

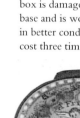

▲ TORTOISESHELL BOXES
Tortoiseshell, molded by heat and pressure, was often used for making small boxes during the 18th and 19th centuries. This 19th century cigar case is decorated with stellar *piqué*, (an inlay of gold or silver). $300–500+

◀ TUNBRIDGE WARE
Tunbridge ware decoration was mostly made, as the name suggests, in the Tunbridge Wells area of Kent. The technique involved making pictures from long strands of differently colored woods which were glued together, and sliced transversely into thin sheets. Value depends on the fineness of the decoration; this one is of average quality. $400–600

VINTAGE FOUNTAIN PENS

Condition is the prime factor in the value of old pens, as they can be expensive to restore, so check carefully for signs of excessive wear. Avoid pens with cracks or replaced parts which have been forced or glued to the body. Pens in mint condition are worth four or five times as much as worn ones.

> **PREMIER PENS**
>
> Quality pens (before 1945) by these makers are especially desirable: Parker ● Conklin ● Waterman ● Montblanc ● Mabie Todd Co. (Swan) ● Wahl-Eversharp ● Sheaffer ● Dunhill-Namiki.

1 Pens marked as a calendar with dates and the seven days of the week were only made by Waterman. This was made in 1936 from 9 carat gold. $900–1,350

2 The crescent on the side of this c.1916 gold–plated Conklin was a new design patented by this US maker in 1899 to improve the way the pen was filled. $300–500

3 This c.1905 silver Swan eyedropper is especially valuable because of its high quality scroll and lozenge decoration. $600–900

4 It probably took as long as 2 weeks to decorate this c.1935 Dunhill-Namiki pen with high–quality lacquer decoration. $1,500–3,000

5 The Lily pattern decorating this pen is one of the rarest designs used by Swan during the early years of the 20th century. $2,000

6 This Montblanc pen, made c.1924, is of a fairly standard design, but is still worth $1,200–1,600, because the case is decorated with gold overlay.

7 Although this gold–plated Conklin filigree pen made c.1918 is a more common type than No. 2, it's in a larger size so would still be worth $900–1,500

8 There are fakes of this unusual "spider's web" c.1924 Montblanc Model 1M but they are usually suspiciously "new" in appearance. $2,000–3,000

9 This "Smallest pen in the World" was a novelty made by Waterman c.1910-15; one was made for Queen Mary's Dolls House. $2,000

● Waterman also produced a massive No.20 safety pen. They also reportedly made similar cases fitted with flasks for hiding whiskey during Prohibition.

TRIBAL ART

The strong images and primitive shapes which characterize tribal art have enjoyed a huge increase in popularity in recent years. However, because prices have risen steeply and the demand for genuine old pieces has greatly outstripped supply, there has also been a huge increase in fake pieces on the market. The many fakes produced in America, Africa and the Far East for the tourist market can be very hard to identify, so if you're an inexperienced collector, buy from a reputable source who can guarantee the age of any piece purporting to be old.

Provenance is important to the value of tribal art. The most desirable pieces are those which have at some time been used for their intended domestic, ceremonial or ritual purpose, and were collected by colonial settlers or missionaries during the 19th or early 20th century.

WHAT TO LOOK FOR
- Northwest coast carvings.
- Navajo classic blankets.
- Clubs from Pacific Islands.
- African tribal jewellery.
- Benin bronzes – often faked, so beware.
- Baule masks from the Ivory Coast.

◄ MASKS
Masks are one of the most popular collecting areas of tribal art; many were used in tribal ceremonies and have symbolic significance. This Sepik mask is particularly valuable because of its provenance: it comes from the collection of Frank Wonder who acquired it on an expedition to New Guinea in the 1920s.
$7,500-10,000

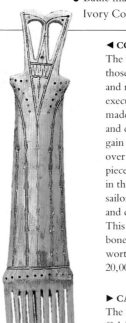

◄ CONDITION
The finest pieces are those of elegant form and masterful execution. Objects made for domestic and ceremonial use gain a certain patina over time. Many pieces were collected in the 19th century by sailors, missionaries and colonial settlers. This Eskimo walrus bone comb (9½in), is worth $15,000–20,000.

▶ CALABASHES
The Hawaiian Calabash bowl, was a status symbol made from the finest quality wood and

passed down through families. Before the early 19th century they were hand-carved, later examples were made

on a lathe. Because the elaborate butterfly repairs on this one enhance its aesthetic appeal, it's worth $5,000-7,000.

ANTIQUITIES

If, like many collectors, you've always assumed that antiquities are prohibitively expensive, you may be surprised to find out that the average auction of antiquities contains many objects priced at hundreds rather than thousands of dollars. Nonetheless, antiquities have long been sought after, and faking in one form or another has existed throughout the centuries. There is also the added complication of export laws which exist in most countries where antiquities originate. Collectors should always make sure the piece is being sold legally.

BEWARE
- Antiquities are fragile and condition affects value, but some damage is to be expected – be suspicious of anything which seems too perfect.
- Avoid objects with heavy restoration – particularly if it is on the face of a piece of sculpture or a painting.
- Avoid bronzes which have become badly corroded – their detail may have been irreparably damaged.

▲ EGYPTIAN ANTIQUITIES
Egyptian antiquities can be extremely valuable but there are exceptions. This red-ware vase dates from 3,500-3,200BC and is worth about $300. Other inexpensive antiquities include:
- small Egyptian limestone carvings
- roman terracotta oil lamps
- small examples of Cypriot pottery.

▼ ROMAN GLASS
It might seem inconceivable that glass from the 2nd century can be no more expensive than that of the 18th century, but this is often the case. These vases illustrate the subtle colors and iridescence typical of much Roman glass and are worth between $300-800 each.

REMEMBER...
If you have any doubts about the legality or authenticity of a piece consult museum experts.

◀ GREEK POTTERY
Valuable Greek pottery is often decorated with scenes from mythology. This Attic (made in Athens) black-figure amphora (two-handled urn) dates from c.510-500BC, and shows Peleus chasing Thetis. Attic vases with reversed colors (black background and red figures) are known as red-figure vases. $12,000-18,000

PART 4

FACT FILE

ABOVE A SELECTION OF INVALUABLE MILLER'S
COLLECTOR'S GUIDES.

LEFT RECORDING PRICES AT BERMONDSEY
ANTIQUES MARKET, LONDON.

WHERE TO SEE

There are many places where you can see and study antiques. Some of the major collections found in museums historical societies and historic houses open to the public are listed below.

CALIFORNIA
Los Angeles County
Museum of Art
5905 Wilshire Blvd
Los Angeles
CA 90036
(213) 857-6111
Asian Art Museum of
San Francisco
The Avery Brundage
Collection
Golden Gate Park
San Francisco
CA 94118
(415) 668-8921
CONNECTICUT
Wadsworth
Atheneum
600 Main St.
Hartford
CT 06103
(203) 278-2670
Yale University Art
Gallery
1111 Chapel St.
York
New Haven
CT 06520
(203) 432-0600
DELAWARE
Winterthur Museum
and Gardens
Winterthur
Delaware 19735
(302) 888-3600
**DISTRICT OF
COLUMBIA**
National Museum of
American History
Smithsonian
Institution

Constitution Ave.
between 12th and 14th
Sts.
(202) 357-1300
The Renwick Gallery
National Museum of
American Art
Smithsonian
Institution
Pennsylvania Ave. at
17th St., NW
Washington D.C.
(202) 357-2700
National Museum of
African Art
Smithsonian
Institution
950 Independence
Ave., SW
Washington D.C.
20560
Arthur M. Sackler
Gallery
Smithsonian
Institution
1050 Independence
Ave., SW
Washington D.C.
20560
(202) 357-2700
Textile Museum 2320
S. St., NW
Washington D.C.
20008
(202) 667-0441
GEORGIA
High Museum of Art
1280 Peachtree St.,
NE
Atlanta
GA 30349

(404) 892-4444
ILLINOIS
Art Institute of
Chicago
Michigan Ave. at
Adams St.
Chicago
ILL 60603
(312) 443-3600
MARYLAND
Baltimore Museum
of Art
Art Museum Drive
Baltimore
Md. 21218
(410) 396-7100
Walters Art Gallery
640 N. Charles St.
Baltimore
Md. 21201
(410) 547-9000
**MASSACHU-
SETTS**
Hancock Shaker
Village
Albany Road
Route 20
P.O. Box 898
Pittsfield
Ma. 02102
(413) 443-0100
Historic Deerfield
The Street
Box 321
Deerfield
Ma. 01342
(413) 774-5581
Museum of Fine Arts
Boston
46 Huntington Ave.
Boston
Ma. 02115
(617) 267-9300
Old Sturbridge
Village
1 Old Sturbridge
Village Road

Sturbridge
Ma. 015662
(508) 347-3362
Peabody Essex
Museum East India
Square
Liberty and Essex
Sts.
Salem
Ma. 01970
(508) 745-9500
Society for the
Preservation of New
England Antiquities
(SPNEA) Harrison
Gray Otis House
141 Cambridge St.
Boston
Ma. 02114
(617) 227-3956
MICHIGAN
The Detroit Institute
of Arts
5200 Woodward Ave.
Detroit
MI 48202
(313) 833-7900
The Henry Ford
Museum and
Greenfield Village
20900 Oakwood
Dearborn MI
(313) 271-1620
MINNESOTA
Minneapolis Institute
of Arts
2400 Third Ave.
South Minneapolis
Minn. 55404
(612) 870-3200
MISSOURI
Nelson-Atkins
Museum of Art
4525 Oak St.
Kansas City
Mo. 64111
(816) 561-4000

Saint Louis Art
Museum
One Fine Arts Drive
Forest Park
St. Louis
Mo. 63110
**NEW
HAMPSHIRE**
Currier Gallery of
Art
19 Orange St.
Manchester
N.H. 03801
(603) 669 6144
Strawberry Banke
Marcy St.
P.O. Box 300
Portsmouth
N.H. 03801
(603) 433-1100
NEW JERSEY
Newark Museum
49 Washington St.
Newark
N.J. 07101
(201) 596-6550
NEW YORK
Corning Museum of
Glass
One Museum Way
Corning
N.Y. 14830-2253
(607) 937-5371
Brooklyn Museum
200 Eastern Pkwy.
Brooklyn
N.Y. 11236
(718) 638-5000
Cooper Hewitt
National Museum of
Design
Smithsonian
Institution
2 E. 91st St.
New York N.Y.
10128
(212) 860-6868;

Metropolitan
Museum of Art
Fifth Avenue at 82nd
St.
New York N.Y.
10028
(212) 879-5500
Museum of American
Folk Art
Two Lincoln Square
New York
N.Y. 10023-6214
(212) 595-9533
**NORTH
CAROLINA**
Museum of Early
Southern Decorative
Arts (MESDA)
924 South Main St.
N.C. 27101
(919) 514-4900
OHIO
Cleveland Museum
of Art
11150 East Blvd.
Cleveland
Ohio 44106
(216) 421-7340
PENNSYLVANIA
Heritage Center
Center Square
13 W. King St.
Lancaster
Pa. 17603
(717) 299-6440
Philadelphia Museum
of Art
26th St. and
Benjamin Franklin
Parkway
Philadelphia
Pa. 19130
(215) 763-8100
University Museum
of Archeology and
Anthropology
University of

Pennsylvania
33rd and Spruce St.
Philadelphia
Pa. 19104
(215) 8989-4000
Carnegie Museum of
Art
4400 Forbes Ave.
Pittsburgh
Pa. 15213
(412) 622-3131
RHODE ISLAND
Museum of Art
Rhode Island School
of Design
224 Benefit St.
Providence
R.I. 02903
(401) 454-6500
The Preservation
Society of Newport
County
P.O. Box 510
Newport R.I. 02840
(401) 847-1000
**SOUTH
CAROLINA**
Charlestown
Museum
764 Meeting St. (and
three historic houses)
Charleston S.C.
(803) 722-2996
TEXAS
Dallas Museum of
Art
1717 N. Harwood
Dallas
Texas 75291
(214) 922-1200
Bayou Bend Museum
and Gardens
1 Westcott Houston
Texas (part of the
Museum of Fine Arts
Houston)
(713) 520-2600

VERMONT
Shelburne Museum
Route 7
Burlington
VT. 05482
(802) 985-3346
VIRGINIA
The Chrysler
Museum
24 W. Olney Road
Norfolk
Va. 23510-1567
(804) 622-1211
Virginia Museum of
Fine Arts
2800 Grove Ave.
Richmond
Va. 23221-2466
(804) 367-0844
Colonial
Williamsburg
P.O. Box C
Williamsburg
Va. 23187
(804) 229-1000
WISCONSIN
Milwaukee Art
Museum
750 N. Lincoln
Memorial Dr.
Milwaukee
Wis. 53202
(414) 224-3200
CANADA
Musé des Beaux-Arts
de Montreal
1380 Sherbrook St.
West
Montreal, Quebec
Canada H6 2T9
(514) 285-1600
National Gallery of
Canada
380 Sussex Dr.
Ottawa, Ontario
Canada K1N 9N4
(613) 990-1985

WHERE TO BUY

Major Auction Houses

Ronald Bourgeault Northeast Auctions
P.O. Box 363
Hampton
NH 03842
(603) 926-9800

Butterfield and Butterfield
220 San Bruno Ave. at 15th St.
San Francisco
CA 94103
(415) 861-7500

Butterfield LA
7601 Sunset Blvd.
Los Angeles
CA 90046
(213) 850-7500

Christie's
502 Park Ave.
New York
NY 10022
(212) 546-1000

Christie's East
219 E. 67th St.
New York
NY 10021
(212) 606-0400

William Doyle Galleries
175 E. 87th St.
New York
NY 10128
(212) 427-2730

Garth's Auctions
2690 Stratford Road
Box 369
Delaware
Ohio 43015
(614) 362-4771

Goldberg Auction Galleries Inc.
547 Baronne St.
New Orleans
LA 70176

(504) 592-2300
Leslie Hindman Auctioneers
215 West Ohio St.
Chicago
ILL 60610
(312) 670-0010

Metropolitan Arts and Antiques Pavillion
110 W. 19th St.
New York
NY 10011
(212) 463-0200

Pook and Pook
P.O. Box 268
Downingtown
PA 19335
(215) 269-0695

Skinner Inc.
Route 117
Bolton
MA 01451
(508) 779-6241

Skinner Boston
63 Park Plaza
Boston
MA 02116
(617) 350-5400

Sotheby's
1334 York Avenue
New York
NY 10021
(212) 606-7000

Theriault's The Doll Masters
P.O. Box 151
Annapolis
MD 21404
1-800-638-0422

Weschler & Son
909 E, St. NW
Washington D.C.
20004
(202) 628-1281

Major Antiques Shows

January
Heart of Country Antiques Show
Opryland Hotel
Nashville, TN
(314) 862-1091

Miami National Antiques Show
Radisson Expo. Center
Miami, FL
(301) 738-1966

Washington Antiques Show
Omni Shorham Hotel
2500 Calvert St. NW
Washington D.C.
(703) 765-3469

February
Stella's Manhattan Triple Pier Exposition (and November)
Piers 88, 90, 92 W. 55th St.
New York, NY
(201) 384-0011

March
Atlantique City
Spring Festival (and Atlantique Holiday Fair October)
Covention Center Boardwalk
Atlantic City, NJ
(609) 926-1800

Connecticut Spring Antiques Show
University of Hartford's Sports Center
200 Bloomfield Ave.
West Hartford, CT
(207) 767-3967

Ephemera Society of

America Fair and Exhibition
Hyatt Regency Hotel
Old Greenwich, CT
(518) 674-2673

Wendy's Armory Antiques Show
(and December)
Seventh Regiment Armory
67th St. and Park Ave.
New York, NY
(914) 698-3442

Wilton Historical Society Show
Wilton High School Field House
Wilton, CT
(203) 762-7257

Winnetka Antique Show
Winnetka Community House
Winnetka
IL 60093
(708) 446-9537

April
Philadelphia Antiques Show
103rd Engineers Armory
33rd and Market Sts.
Philadelphia, PA
(215) 387-3500

Southport-Westport Antiques Show
Fairfield County Hunt Club
Westport, CT
(203) 259-7610

May
Brimfield Markets
(and July, September)
Route 20
Brimfield, MA
(413) 245-9556

June
Farmington Antiques
Weekend (and
September)
Farmington Polo
Grounds
near Hartford, CT
(508) 839-9735
August
New Hampshire
Antiques Dealers
Association Show
Center of New
Hampshire Holiday
Inn
700 Elm St.
Manchester, NH
(603) 286-7506
Papermania Plus
Hartford Civic
Center
Hartford, CT
(203) 529-7582
Santa Fe Indian
Market
The Plaza
Santa Fe, NM
(505) 984-6760
Vermont Antiques
Dealers Association
Show
Stratton Mountain
Base Lodge
Bondville, VT
(802) 365-7574
September
A.D.A. Annual
Antiques Show
Westchester County
Center
White Plains, NY
(508) 463-4325
Baltimore Summer
Antiques Fair &
Antiquarian Book
Fair
Baltimore Covention

Center
Baltimore, Maryland
(301) 738-1966
Theta Charity
Antiques Show
Astro Hall
Houston, Texas
(713) 622-5168
October
Connecticut Antiques
Show
University of
Hartford's Sports
Center
200 Bloomfield Ave.
West Hartford, CT
(212) 777-5218
Ellis Memorial
Hospital Show
The Cyclorama
539 Tremont St.
Boston, MA
(703) 765-3469
Fall Antiques Show
Pier 92
W. 52nd St.
New York, NY
(212) 777-5218
International Fine Art
and Antiques Dealers
Show
Seventh Regiment
Armory
New York, NY 10021
Pappabello Fall
Antiques Show &
Sale
Richfield Coliseum
Cleveland, Ohio
(301) 738-1966
San Francisco Fall
Antiques Show
Fort Mason Center
Festival Pavillion
San Francisco, CA
(415) 921-1411
November

Delaware Antiques
Show
DuPont Country
Club
Wilmington,
Delaware
(302) 888-4600
Modernism: A
Century of Style and
Design
Seventh Regiment
Armory
New York, NY
(212) 777-5218
Associations
Antiques Council
P.O. Box 574
Southport
CT 06490
(203) 259-7610
A.A.D.L.A. Art &
Antique Dealers
League of America
353 E. 78th St.,
New York
NY 10021
A.D.A. Antique
Dealers Association
of America
Box 632
Newburyport
MA 01950
(508) 463-4325
N.A.A.D.A.A.
National Antique &
Art Dealers
Association of
America
15 E. 57th St.
New York
NY 10022
P.A.D.A.C.
Professional Art
Dealers Association
of Canada
296 Richmond St. W.
Toronto

Ontario
M5V 1X2
Canada
(416) 979-1276
**Antiques Markets
and Group Shops**
The Annex
26th St. and 6th Ave.
New York, NY
(212) 243-5343
Ann Arbor Antiques
Market
5055 Ann Arbor-
Saline Rd.
Ann Arbor MI
M. Brusher
P.O. Box 1512
Ann Arbor
MI 48106
(313) 662-9453
Antiques Associates
at West Townsend
473 Main St.
West Townsend
MA 01474
(508) 597-8084
The Garage
112 W. 25th St.
New York, NY
(212) 647-0707
Renniger's
Extravaganza
27 Noble St.
Kutztown, PA
(717) 385-0104
Renniger's
Adamstown
Extravaganzas
Exit 21 PA Turnpike
Route 272
Adamstown PA
(717) 336-2177
York Antiques
Gallery
Route 1
York, Maine
(207) 363-5002

WHAT TO READ

GENERAL

Time Life
   Encyclopedia of
   Collectibles (1978–
   1980)
Fleming, John and
   Honour, Hugh
   "Dictionary of
   Decorative Arts"
   (1977)
Kaye Myrna "Fake
   Fraud or Genuine?"
   (1897)

FURNITURE

Barquist, David
   "American Tables
   and Looking
   Glasses I at Yale
   University" (1992)
Beckerdite, Luke
   (Ed.) "American
   Furniture" (1993)
Bowman and
   Heckscher,
   "American
   Rococo" (1992)
Cooper, Wendy A.
   "Classical Taste in
   America, 1800–
   1840" (1995)
Chinnery, Victor
   "Oak Furniture,
   the British
   Tradition" (1979)
Downs Joseph
   "American
   Furniture Queen
   Anne and
   Chippendale
   Periods in the I
   Winterthur
   Museum" (1952)
Fairbanks, Jonathan
   and Bidwell,
   Elizabeth
   "American
   Furniture 1620 to

the Present" (1981)
Fales, Dean A.
   "American Painted
   Furniture, 1660–
   1880" (1972)
Forman, Benno
   "American Seating
   Furniture, 1630–
   1730" (1988)
Heckscher, Morrison
   "American
   Furniture in the
   Metropolitan
   Museum Late
   Colonial Queen
   Anne and
   Chippendale"
   (1985)
Jobe, Brock,
   "Portsmouth
   Furniture" (1993)
Jobe, Brock with
   Kaye, Myrna
   "New England
   Furniture, the
   Colonial Era"
   (1985)
Kirk, John
   "American Chairs,
   Queen Anne and
   Chippendale"
   (1972), "American
   Furniture and the
   British Tradition to
   1830" (1982),
   "Early American
   Furniture" (1967)
Montgomery,
   Charles F.
   "American Federal
   Furniture in the I
   Winterthur
   Museum" (1966)
Puig, Francis J. and
   Conforti, Michael
   "The American
   Craftsman and the

European Tradition
   1620-1820" (1989).
Reiman, Timothy D.
   and Burks, Jean M.
   "The Complete
   Book of Shaker
   Furniture" (1993)
Sack, Albert "Fine
   Points of American
   Furniture" (1993)
Santore, Charles
   "The Windsor
   Style" (2 vols.
   1982, 1987)
Ward, Gerald W.R.
   "American Case
   Furniture I at Yale
   University" (1988)
Weidman, Gregory,
   R. "Furniture in
   Maryland 1740–
   1949" (1984)

CERAMICS

Frelinghuysen, Alice
   Cooney "American
   Porcelain" (1989)
Cushion, John and
   Margaret "A
   Collector's History
   of British
   Porcelain" (1992)
Guide Halfpenny, Pat
   "English
   Earthenware
   Figures, 1740 to
   1840" (1992)
Evans, Paul "Art
   Pottery in the
   United States"
   (1987)
Godden, Geoffrey
   "Guide to English
   Porcelain" (1992),
   "Encyclopedia of
   British Pottery &
   Porcelain
   Manufacturers"

(1988)
Levitt, Elaine,
   "History of
   American
   Ceramics, 1607 to
   Present" (1988)
Lewis, John and
   Griselda ""Pratt
   Ware", 1780–1840"
   (revised 1993)
Pugh, P.D. Gordon,
   "Staffordshire
   Portrait Figures"
   (l971)
Sandon, Henry
   "Worcester
   Porcelain, 1751-
   1851" (1993)

GLASS

McKearin, Helen and
   George, "Two
   Hundred Years of
   American Blown
   Glass" (1949)
McKearin, Helen and
   Wilson, Kenneth
   M. "American
   Bottles & Flasks"
   (1978)
Palmer, Arlene
   "Glass in Early
   America" (1993)

SILVER

Carpenter, Charles,
   H. Jr. "Gorham
   Silver, 1831-1981"
   (1982)
Carpenter, Charles,
   H. Jr. with Mary
   Grace "Tiffany
   Silver', (1978)
Grimwade, Arthur
   "London
   Goldsmiths, 1697-
   1837" (1976)
Kernan, John
   Devereux "Chinese

Export Silver"
(1985)
Rainwater, Dorothy
T. "Encyclopedia
of American Silver
Manufacturers"
(1975)

**RUGS AND
TEXTILES**
Black, David (Ed.)
"World Rugs and
Carpets" (1985)
Kopp, Joel and Kate
"American Hooked
and Sewn Rugs"
(1975)
Ring, Betty
"Girlhood
Embroidery:
American Samplers
& Pictorial
Needlework, 1650
to 1850" (1993)

CLOCKS
Bailey, Chris "Two
Hundred Years of
American Clocks
and Watches"
(1975)
Britten's "Old Clocks
and Watches and
their Makers"
(1973)
Distin, William and
Bishop, Robert
"The American
Clock" (1976)
Palmer, Brooks "The
Book of American
Clocks" (1950)
Robinson, Tom R
The Long Case
Clock" (1993)
Willard, John W. "A
History of Simon
Willard, Inventor
and Clockmaker"

(1968)
**ART NOUVEAU/
ART DECO/
20TH
CENTURY**
Clark, Robert Judson
"The Arts and
Crafts Movement
in America: 1876-
1916" (1972)
Dawes, Nicholas
"Lalique Glass"
(1986)
Duncan, Alistair
"Louis Comfort
Tiffany" (1992)
Ellis, Anita J.
"Rookwood
Pottery" (1992)
Frelinghuysen, Alice
C. and others "In
Pursuit, of Beauty:
Americans and the
Aesthetic
Movement" (1987)
Hanks, A. David
"The Decorative
Designs of Frank
Lloyd Wright"
(1977)
Hiesinger, Katheryn
B. and Marcus,
George
"Landmarks of
Twentieth Century
Design" (1993)
Kaplan, Wendy "The
Art that is Life:
The Arts and
Crafts Movement
in America" (1987)
**BEARS, DOLLS
AND TOYS**
Barenholtz, Bernard
and McClintock,
Inez "American
Antique Toys"

(1980)
Bauman, Paul
"Collecting
Antique Marbles"
(2nd edition, 1991)
Cieslik, Jurgen, and
Marianne "The
German Doll
Encyclopedia"
(1985)
Coleman, E.D. and
E.J. "The
Collector's
Encyclopedia of
Dolls" (vols. I and
II, 1968)
Davidson, Al "Penny
Lane Antique
Mechanical Toy
Banks" (1987)
Gottschalk, Lillian
"American Toy
Cars and Trucks"
(1985)
Keane, Martin J.
"Classic Rods and
Rod Makers',
(1976)
Kurt, Henry and
Ehrlich, Burt R.
"The Art of the
Toy Soldier" (1987)
Lesser, Robert "A
Celebration of
Comic Art and
Memorabilia"
(1975)
O'Brien, Richard,
"The Story of
American Toys"
(1990)
**OTHER COLLEC-
TIBLES**
Dike, Catherine
"Cane Curiosa"
(1983)
Bennion, Elizabeth

"Antique Medical
Instruments" (1979)
Crossman, Carl "The
Decorative Arts of
the China Trade"
Epstein, Diana, and
Safro, Millicent
"Buttons" (1991)
Gentle, Rupert and
Feild, Rachel
"English Domestic
Brass 1690-1810"
(1975)
Garvan, Beatrice B.
"The Pennsylvania
German
Collection,
Philadelphia
Museum of Art"
(1982)
Kay, Hilary "Rock
and Roll
Collectables"
(1992)
Lippman, Paul
"American
Typewriters: A
Collector's
Encyclopedia"
(1991)
Olman, John, and
Morton, W. "The
Encyclopedia of
Golf Collectibles"
(1985)
Schneider, Stuart and
Fishler, George
"Fountain Pens and
Pencils: The
Golden Age of
Writing
Instruments" (1990)
Turner, Anthony
"Early Scientific
Instruments" (1987)

GLOSSARY

Acanthus Classical ornament based on the scalloped leaf of the acanthus plant used on a wide variety of objects.

Acid cutting A method of decorating glass where objects were coated with an acid-resistant substance, such as wax; a design was scratched on the wax with a steel point and fixed by dipping the object in acid.

Air twist stem On drinking glasses and other glassware, a stem decorated with spiral filaments of hollow glass.

Ambrotype A photograph made by exposing a glass plate treated with light-sensitive wet collodion. The negative was made positive by backing with black paper or paint (see p150).

Appliqué In textiles, stitching small patches of fabric to a base fabric to make a design.

Arita An important center for Japanese porcelain production, and a term used to describe one distinctive type of Japanese porcelain made in the area (see p67).

Armorial An engraved crest and/or coat of arms.

Arts & Crafts A late 19th century artistic movement led by William Morris in England and Gustav Stickley in America, which advocated a return to medieval standards of crafts-manship and simplicity of design.

Automata A term covering a variety of mechanical toys with moving parts, popular during the 18th and 19th centuries.

Baluster Vase-shaped form with a bulbous base, narrow waist and slightly flared neck. Commonly used on silverwares, ceramics and stems of drinking glasses.

Ball and claw A furniture foot in the shape of an animal's paw grasping on ball. Used on cabriole legs.

Basalt Unglazed black stoneware, developed by Wedgwood.

Bergère French style armchair with wood frame and upholstered sides.

Berlin Woolwork Amateur embroidery using colored wools on a canvas grid.

Biscuit Unglazed porcelain, fired only once.

Blue-dash charger A delftware dish decorated with a border of blue brush strokes.

Blueing A decorative heat treatment applied to metal which also protected it from rust.

Bone china Porcelain made by the addition of large quantities of bone ash.

Bracket clock A type of spring-driven clock, designed to stand on a shelf, table or bracket.

Britannia metal An alloy of tin, antimony and copper, a light weight, whiter pewter used during the 19th century.

Cabriole leg A furniture leg in the shape of an elongated S.

Cameo glass Wares made by combining two or more layers of differently colored glass which was carved to made a design in relief.

Case furniture Furniture intended as a receptacle, such as a chest of drawers.

Chasing A method of decorating silver from the outside using a hammer and chasing tools including punches.

Chinoiserie European Oriental-style figures and scenes used to decorate many different types of objects.

Creamware Lead glazed creamy-white earthenware.

Cornice The projecting molding at the top of tall furniture; border between wall and ceiling.

Credenza A long side-cabinet with glazed or solid doors.

Cross-banding A veneered border at right-angles to the main veneer (see p44).

Cruet A frame for holding casters and bottles for condiments.

Davenport A small writing desk with a sloped top above a case of drawers.

Delftware Tin-glazed earthenware from England or the Low Countries.

Distressed A term used to describe an object that has been artificially aged.

Drum table A circular table with a frieze containing drawers supported by a central pedestal.

Ebonized Stained black in imitation of ebony.

Étui A small case for scissors and other small implements.

Faïence Tin-glazed earthenware from France.

Façon de Venise Glassware imitating Venetian styles.

Flatback Ceramic portrait figures with flat, undecorated backs, designed to stand against a wall or on a mantelpiece (see p81).

Flatware Any flat or shallow tableware, such as knives, forks, spoons and serving pieces for the dining table.

Gesso A plaster-like substance used as a substitute for carved wood, or as a base for painted or gilded decoration.

Hallmark The marks stamped on silver or gold objects when passed at assay (the test for quality).

Hard-paste porcelain Porcelain made using the ancient Chinese combination of kaolin and petuntse.

Imari A type of Japanese porcelain with red, blue, gold and green brocade-like decoration, exported through the port of Imari and widely copied.

Intaglio Incised gemstone or any incised decoration; the opposite of carving in relief.

Istoriato Narrative scenes painted on Italian *maiolica*.

Jacobite glass Wine glasses engraved with symbols of the Jacobites (supporters of Prince Charles Edward Stuart's claim to the throne).

Japanning European imitation of Oriental lacquer (see p58).

Jasperware A hard fine-grained colored stoneware decorated with high relief white garlands, developed by Wedgwood.

Joined Term used to describe furniture made by a joiner.

Kakiemon Sparsely-decorated Japanese porcelain made by the Kakiemon family in the 17th century. The style was much imitated by later potters.

Kaolin A fine white granite clay used in hard-paste porcelain, also known as China clay.

Kashan Rug-making center in Southern Iran, noted for high quality products.

Kazak Rugs from central Caucasus, usually decorated with distinctive geometric designs.

Kelim A flat woven rug with no pile.

Kneehole desk A writing desk with drawers on either side and a central recess.

Ladder back A chair with a back made from a series of horizontal slats between the two vertical uprights.

Ladik A Turkish prayer rug, usually decorated with a niche and stylized tulip flowers.

Lap joint In silverware most frequently used to solder a finial to the stem of an apostle spoon.

Lead Crystal Glass containing lead oxide which gives extra weight and brilliance.

Library table A rectangular table with frieze drawers, end supports and a central stretcher.

Linen press A case piece with both drawers and cupboard drawers.

loaded Another term for weighted, when a silver candlestick has been filled with pitch or plaster to give it stability.

long arm A firearm with a long barrel.

longcase clock A tall clock with a case consisting of weights and pendulum and a hood housing dial and movement; called a tall case in the USA.

Lowboy A dressing table, often made

en suite with a highboy (high chest) in the USA.

Maiolica Tin-glazed earthenwares from Italy.

Majolica Victorian earthenware often with relief decoration fired to the biscuit stage and then covered with an opaque background glaze of tin or lead enamel and decorated in brightly colored metallic-oxide glazes and refired.

Marquetry Design formed from veneers of different colored woods.

Marriage The joining together of two previously unrelated parts to form a whole.

Mihrab A niche with a pointed arch, seen on prayer rugs.

Millefiori Glass made by fusing different colored rods of glass which resembles "a thousand flowers"; used for paper-weights.

Monteith Large silver bowl, with a scalloped rim.

Mortise and tenon Type of joint used in furniture; the mortise is a cavity,

into which the shaped tenon fits and is held in place by pegs.

Mother-of-pearl Slices of shell often used for decorative inlay.

Motif A decorative detail, often repeated to form a pattern.

Mystery clock A clock of novel form in which the movement is ingeniously hidden.

Occasional table Small, easily portable table.

Octant Device made from one eighth of a circle, used for measuring angular distance.

Opaque twist A white or colored twist of glass contained in the stem of a drinking glass.

Ormolu Gilt bronze or brass, generally 18th century. Hardware furniture generally has mercury gilding as distinguished from gilt bronze dipped in acid and lacquered.

Overglaze A second glaze laid over a first and refired; also known as enamelling.

Pad foot On

furniture, a rounded foot, resembling that of an animal.

Palmette A stylized palm-leaf motif, often used to decorate Oriental carpets and furniture.

Papier-mâché Paper pulp combined with glue, used to make small objects such as boxes and trays; also applied over a metal frame to make larger pieces of furniture, such as tables and chairs.

Parcel gilt Wood with gilt or silver gilt parts.

Parian Fine white biscuit porcelain resembling marble; popular from mid-19th century.

Parquetry Decorative veneers of wood laid in a geometric pattern.

Pate The Crown of a doll's head.

Patina The term used to describe the surface color and sheen of furniture, silver and other objects which is built up from years of use.

Petuntse China stone; a granite used to make hard paste porcelain.

Plate A generic term for gold and silver vessels, not to be confused with Sheffield Plate or plated wares.

Porringer A two-handled dish, sometimes with a lid, originally for holding porridge or broth. Generally made from silver and pewter.

Pressed glass Glass wares formed by mechanical pressure applied to molten glass in a mold.

Quadrant A quarter circle, marked with degrees of a circle and with a weighted line or pointer, used as a navigational aid.

Quarter-veneered Four pieces of identical veneer, which are laid opposite each other to create a decorative effect.

Quartetto tables A set of four graduating matching tables, that can be stored inside each other.

Rack The structure, comprising several shelves, at the top of some dressers.

Refectory table Term used to describe the long

rectangular dining tables of the 17th century and later.

Reproduction A piece which is a copy of an earlier design.

"Right" Dealers' term for something which is genuine and authentic, as opposed to "wrong", which means it is faked, altered or restored.

Saber A curving sword used mainly by cavalrymen.

Saber leg An elegant outward curving leg, associated with 19th century furniture.

Sampler Needlework pictures; incorporating different stitches and designs.

Scent bottle A small portable flask, often of flattened pear shape.

Settle A long wooden bench with high back and arms.

Sextant Navigational instrument, formed from one sixth of a circle.

Sgraffito Decorative technique whereby the surface has been covered with slip and the design incised to show a contrasting color beneath.

Shako A 19th century military cap of conical or cylindrical shape with a peak.

Shiraz Center of distribution in central Iran for nomadic rugs decorated with simple geometric designs.

Slip Clay mixed with water, often used to decorate pottery.

Snuffer Cone-shaped metal implement used to extinguish candles.

Socket A plate or bracket on the wall to which lights or candle-holders could be attached. Also used to describe the wall lights themselves.

Sterling silver Silver of 925 or 1000 parts pure silver, the standard for hall marked English silver and American silver marked "Sterling."

Stock The wooden part of a firearm to which the metal barrel and firing mechanism are attached.

Tester Wooden or textile canopy over a bed, it may cover only half the bed and be supported by two or four posts; hence full tester or half tester beds.

Train A set of cog wheels and pinions in a clock movement.

Treen Small wooden domestic objects, sometimes in the shape of fruit.

Tunbridge ware Objects decorated with pictures or designs made from bundles of different colored wood cut in sections.

Tureen A large bowl on a foot used for serving soup.

Turned furniture Pieces made from lathe turned wood.

Veneer A thin sheet of wood applied to furniture for decorative effect.

Vesta case A small box for vestas (early matches) called match safes in the US.

Vinaigrette A small portable container containing a sponge scented with vinegar.

Warp Threads used to make the foundation of a textile running from one end to the other on carpets forming fringes in ceramics.

Weft Cross wise threads, which run at right angles to the warp.

Wet plate camera Earliest form of camera, often made of brass-bound mahogany.

Whatnot Tall stand of four or five display shelves and sometimes a drawer in the base.

Windsor furniture Indoor/outdoor furniture, primarily chairs with solid plank seats, turned legs attached through holes in the seat, as were the spindles which form the back which are held in place with steam bent hoops, arm rails or crests. Usually with a saddle seat and simple turned legs.

Wine funnel Cone, with a spout and often a matching dish for filtering and decanting wine.

Wing chair Upholstered chair with a high back and wing-like side projections.

X-frame The X-shaped construc-tion of some chairs and stools.

INDEX

ACKNOWLEDGMENTS

The publishers would like to thank the following:
Cover t**IT, tr**PM, **bl**SNY, **br**SNY, **c**CNY, **b**SNY;**2**vaseSL,spoon CS,figuresCL, paperweightCL,longcase SL,shoesCNY,clockSL, vaseSL,tobyjugCSK, chairSL,tureenSL,bureau CL,rugSL;**3**bowlSL, trainsCSK,dollSL,caster SL,stoolSL,glassCL;**10**P; **11**SL,**12**CSK;**13t**CSK, **b**B;**14**S;**15**B;**16**MM;**17** AP;**18**P;**19**P;**20**NEC;**21**P; **22**tG,**bl**MM,**br**BR;**23** BR;**24**BR;**26**KSA;**27**CC; **28**B;**29**B;**32**DS;**34**WD; **35**SR;**36**SP;**37**CL;**41**MB; **42**tSL,**b**WB;**43**JGM;**44** CNY;**45**tSL,**b**LB;**46** r**WB;**47**tl**WB,**c**Hum,**bl** WB,**br**LB;**50**PJ;**51** c**Ren,**b**WB;**52**SL;**53** t**MB,**ct**WB,**cb**JGM, **b**Hum;**54**tlSL,**tr**SL,**cl** SL,**bl**SL,**55**SL;**56b**WB; **57t**Wil,**c**SL,**b**Hock;**58bl** RD,**r**SL;**59bl**LB,**r**SL;**60** tlCL,**cl**Wak;**61l**SL,**c**WB, **b**CL;**62**S;**63l**CL,**r**CL;**65** tCL;**66**SL,**bl**SL,**br**CSK; **67c**SL,**br**SL;**68** lCNY,**c**SL,**r**CNY;**69** lCL,**c**SL,**r**CL;**70l**SL; **71**SL;**72l**SL,**r**CL,**bc**SL; **75**tSL,**cr**SZ;**74**clCL,**cr** SL,**b**CL;**75**t×2SL;**76**tCL, **b**SL;**77**CL;**78**tCSK,**79** c**MB;**80**tMB,**c**SL, **b**SNY;**81l**SL,**c**MB, r**Den;**84**tlCNY,**c**CNY, **bc**CNY;**85**SL×2;**86l**CL, r**CNY;**87**tSL,**cl**CNY, **cr**CNY;**88c**SL, **bl**CNY,**cb**SL,**rb**SL;**89** CNY;**90c**tSL,**cl**CL,**b**SL; **91c**SL,**cr**CNY,**bl**CNY; **92**CSK×3,**bc**MB;**93** CNY×3;**94l**SB,**r**CL;**95**tl SL,**c**SB,**b**CS;**96**CL;**97** clCL,**cr**SL;**98l**CL, rSL;**99**SL×2;**100**CL;**101** tl**H&G,**cr**SL,**b**SL;**102** SL×2**bc**CL;**103**SL;**b**×3 CNY;**106l**SL;**ct**SO,**cr**SL;

107SO;**108c**AW, **cr**SL; **109**SL;**110**SL×3;**111l**CL, **r**SL,**br**DR;**113l**SNY, **r**SNY,**b**SNY;**114l**CL, **r**CL;**115l**Cl,**r**CL,**b**WL; **116**SL×2;**117c**Sl, **b**SNY;**118t**CL,**b**SL;**119** tlCL,**tr**PS,**b**CL;**120** lSL,**r**CNY,**rb**CNY;**121** B×5;**122l**SL,**r**RC,**b**CL; **123c**Cl,**b**CL;**124**tr SL,**cl**SL,**cr**CL;**125** lCNY,**c**CL,**r**CNY;**126** SL;**127t**SL,**r**PC,**b**B;**128** lSL×2,**b**PS;**129c**CSK, **cr**SL,**r**CSK;**132**SL×2;**133** c**SP,**b**SL;**134**SP×3;**135** c**SP,**b**DA;**136**CL;**137** r**CL,**c**CL,**b**MaB;**138**t SL,**c**CSK,**b**SL;**139** r**SL,**c**CNY;**140**CSK;**141** CSK×3;**142**CSK×2, bSL;**143**CSK×3;**144**SL; **145**tCNY,**c**SL,**b**WAL; **146l**SL,**r**SL;**147r**PS,**c**CL, **b**PS;**148**CL×2;**149**CL×3; **150**MB;**151**CSK×3;**152** CSK×2;**153**tlSNY,**tr** CSK,**bl**BB,**btr**CSK;**154** SB×2;**155t&c**SB,**b**SNY; **156l,c,r**CSK,**bl**SL;**157**B; **158bl**C,**br**B,**tr**CL;**159**cl, **cr**CSK,**b**SL;**160**BY

Key
t top, c centre, b bottom, l left, r right

AP Adrian Stemp Antiques, Brighton
AW Anthony Woodburn, Leigh, Kent
B Bonhams
BB Butterfield & Butterfield, Los Angeles, CA
BR Brimfield Markets, Brimfield, MA
C W E Channing & Co., Santa Fe, NM
BY Bermondsey Market
CC The Clock Clinic, Lower Richmond Rd; London
CL Christie's London
CNY Christie's New York

CS Christie's Scotland
CSK Christie's South Kensington
DA Dottie Ayers
Den Richard Dennis, Ilminster
DR Derek Roberts, Tonbridge, Kent
DS Dennis Severs, Folgate Street, London
G The Garage, 12 W. 25th St., New York
H&G Hope & Glory, Kensington Church Street, London
Hock William Hockley Antiques, Petworth, West Sussex
Hum Humphry Antiques, Petworth, West Sussex
JGM John G. Morris Ltd, Petworth, West Sussex
KSA Keith Skeel Antiques, Islington High Street, London
LB Lesley Bragge Antiques, Petworth, West Sussex
MaB Mint and Boxed, London
MB Mitchell Beazley
MM Manhattan Metropolitan Arts and Antiques Pavilion, 110 W. 19th St., New York
NEC British International Antiques Fair, Birmingham
P Portobello Road
PC Phillips, Cardiff
PJ Patrick Jefferson Antiques, 572 Kings Road, London
PM Philadelphia Museum of Art, Philadelphia PA
PS Phillips, London
RC Royal Copenhagen
RD Richard Davidson Antiques, Arundel, West Sussex
Ren Rendall Antiques, London
S Skinner Inc., Bolton, MA
SB Sotheby's

Billingshurst
SL Sotheby's London
SNY Sotheby's New York
SO Strike One, 33 Balcombe St, London
SP Sue Pearson Antiques, 13½ Prince Albert Street; Brighton
SR Sotheby's Restoration Department
SZ Sotheby's Zurich
T Theriault's, P.O. Box 151, Annapolis, MD 21404
Wak Michael Wakelin and Helen Linfield, Petworth, West Sussex
WAL Wallis & Wallis, Lewes, Sussex
WB William Bedford PLC, London
WD West Dean College, West Sussex
Wil T. G. Wilkinson Antiques, Petworth, West Sussex
WL Woven Legends, Philadelphia, PA

Special photography p10-34 Jacqui Hurst and Ian Booth
Illustrations by Karen Cochrane, John Hutchinson, Simon Miller and Vanessa Luff

With special thanks to: Richard Davidson, Leigh Keno, Gordon Lang, Raymond E. Lane, John Wilson, Christopher Hartop, Eric Knowles, John Mighell, Jonathan Snellenburg, Joanna Macfarlane, George Jevremovic, Eric Knowles, Jonathan Hallan, Sue Pearson, Barbara Lauver, Carey Wallace, Dana Hawkes, Alex Crum-Ewing, Katherine Gates, Kevin Conru, Will Channing